Reading is a forceful
weapon against
loneliness"

James Dattie
Author
10. 4. 59

I CYCLED INTO THE ARCTIC CIRCLE

A PEREGRINATION BY
JAMES DUTHIE
& MATT HULSE

The Saltire Society
Matt Hulse
2015

Published by Matt Hulse in association with
The Saltire Society, Scotland
www.saltiresociety.org.uk
www.dummyjim.com

James Duthie's text originally published as *I Cycled into the Arctic Circle* by Arthur H. Stockwell, Ltd., Ilfracombe, 1955 and later by Northern Publishers, Aberdeen, 1957.

Typesetting by Bracketpress

Printed and bound by
CPI Group (UK) Ltd.
Croydon CR0 4YY

ISBN 978-0-85411-121-3

LOTTERY FUNDED

CONTENTS

I CYCLED INTO THE ARCTIC CIRCLE
May to August 1951

APPENDICES

INTRODUCTION

'I reached the Scottish border, where I was happy to see the mighty but humble Scottish people again. I am a Scotsman by birth. Bonnie Scotland!'

This declaration, late in Duthie's journal, is an essential yet insufficient means to explain the affinity between the James' world view, artist Matt Hulse and his film adaptation *Dummy Jim*, and the Saltire Society.

The affinity reaches beyond any sentiment of nationalism. Both James and Matt might be seen as 'Saltire people'.

People who have a hopeful curiosity about the world and its possibilities beyond national boundaries or the limitations of orthodoxy, who nurture a generosity of spirit and a willingness to take others as they find them.

People who believe in everyone's right to a rich cultural life regardless of their economic, social or physical circumstances.

Openness is a recurring theme in the journal as James finds food, shelter and friendship amidst a remarkable range of challenging circumstances. He recounts many positive exchanges with others in the deaf community and the institutions that support them.

More significantly perhaps, Duthie's pedal-powered peregrination through much of Northern Europe brought a lasting impression of his own culture – Scottish, deaf, Presbyterian – to those he met, whether deaf or hearing.

What we would describe now as James' 'disabilities' are the same qualities that lend him a unique perspective, sensibility and courage.

The forthright Aberdeenshire factory worker is not blithely uncritical, however. *I am not so proud of my old school, because I had never been encouraged to seek higher education. What a pity!'*

With the film *Dummy Jim*, Matt offers us a nuanced, multifaceted and astute portrait of his enigmatic, diffident muse. With this new book, he reveals – at times with disconcerting frankness – the complex process at play behind adaptation, filmmaking and creative collaborative practice.

Working on this project for over 15 years, Matt drew courage and inspiration from James. Both the cyclist and the artist's remarkable stamina are perhaps best explained by the film's closing maxim: *He that makes no mistakes, makes nothing.*

In our role as a charity that for 80 years has been celebrating the Scottish imagination, recognising and promoting excellence in Scotland's rich cultural life, it was natural to see James and Matt as remarkable individuals whose life and work merits wider attention.

So dear reader, we are pleased and proud to bring to your attention the new edition of a journal by a remarkable Scotsman as he explores place, culture, education, history, politics, religion and his own potential.

Jim Tough, Executive Director, Saltire Society
Edinburgh, November 2015

FORWARDS

A Note from the Editor

A book is like a piece of rope; it takes on meaning only in connection with the things it holds together.
– Norman Cousins

Can you believe that it took over 15 years to bring this multifarious caper to some sort of satisfactory conclusion?

It felt like it at times, but in pursuit of my goal I was of course never truly alone.

There are many, near and far, that deserve acknowledgement, gratitude and probably also hard cash.

By weaving the valuable contributions of countless individuals into the footnotes of this book, I have done my level best to recognise the efforts of those who found themselves – sometimes reluctantly – sucked into the vortex of *Dummy Jim*.

Unintentionally omitted souls? I seek thy understanding and forgiveness.

Special thanks is overdue to the following: Alan Brown, Lucy Brown, Nick Currey, Ian Dodds, Samuel Dore, James Duthie, Kerry Hopkins, Geoff Huggins, Tishna Molla, Ruth Pendragon, Jeni Reid, Jo Ross, Alice Smith, Eunice Stephen and Emma Turnbull. Pivotal support has come from Bracketpress (Rochdale), Creative Scotland, Flip (Scotland), Inverallochy School, Kindly Folk, The Saltire Society, The Swedenborg Society, the community of Invercairn and of course my own folks.

Better and truer friends it would be hard to find.

Matt Hulse
Beijing, November 2015

This book is dedicated.

JAMES DUTHIE, the author (*with open-neck shirt*), and two friends,
MISS J.A. ELLINGSEN and MR KARL LUNDQVIST, in Narvik, Norway

I CYCLED INTO THE ARCTIC CIRCLE

by

JAMES DUTHIE

Preface

This is an account of my real Continental experiences and of the truth and faith I found in them.

This book, which describes many great universal wonders may, I feel sure, be of interest to read at the fireside in Winter; it will be found interesting for young and old.

I also trust that it may remove many wrong impressions in the public mind as to what the Continental people, both deaf and hearing, really are like. There are many, near and far, that I remember in the spirit of Christian love.

I CYCLED INTO THE ARCTIC CIRCLE

May to August, 1951

MAY 7. I had taken no sleep in my house all night owing to pressure of work in packing all my belongings in canny providence and examining my well-painted bicycle movingly.

Now I was already shaven and neatly dressed; everything was in complete preparation before the commencement of my Continental cycling tour which might take me down to Dover, across the Channel to France, onto Spain and Gibraltar, and finally to Morocco.

My name is James Duthie and I am a deaf mute. As I locked all the doors of the house, Mr. Tait, Mr. Buchan and Mr. Third, well-known Cairnbulg fishermen, came and talked to me. Suddenly they found that I was putting the rucksack, tent, bag, blankets, etc., on my cycle. I opened my red pocket diary and showed them a map of Europe and Northern Africa in which direction my future journey might lie.

At almost 4:30 a.m. I prepared myself to travel a long way to reach Kirkcaldy *via* Lonmay, Mintlaw, Ellon, Aberdeen, Stonehaven, Montrose, Arbroath, Dundee and Cupar.

I was greeted by a well-known yawl fisherman when I passed him near the Cairnbulg Hotel. On my arrival in Kirkcaldy I was invited to stay overnight in the goodly-

7.5.51

This is me - Dummy Jim.

furnished home of Mr. Alex Seath, an old schoolmate of mine, and his parents; I sat enjoying a good conversation with him by the furious coal fire.

I was amazed to learn that the Burntisland Granton ferry boat service had started a new business between the two ferries last month.

* * * *

MAY 8. This is my birthday. At Burntisland ferry I caught a steamer for Granton across the Firth of Forth.

Fifeshire is full of historical interest. During the Reformation struggle in the time of King James the Fifth, Fife was again the chosen battlefield. It was in Fife that Wishart and Patrick Hamilton were burned, that Cardinal Beaton was slain, John Knox began his wonderful career as a preacher and patriot, and that Archbishop Sharpe came to grief on Magus Moor. In short, during these stormy years, the history of Scotland was to a large extent concentrated in the history of Fife.

The Danes landed in Scotland, that is evidenced by the place called Danes' Landing, on the coast of Fife. It is queer for me to hear that many Viking graves have been found on Inchcolm, a rocky island in the Firth of Forth near Aberdour, and far off Burtisland.

The steamer ploughed through the heavy, windblown waves to dock at Granton on the coast of Midlothian. At Leith, near Granton, I visited the home of Mr. John Hume, my old schoolmate, where I had a good tea with his widowed mother. I passed the Royal City of Edinburgh on my way to Dalkeith. It is the seat of the supreme law courts, which are different from those in England, has a university

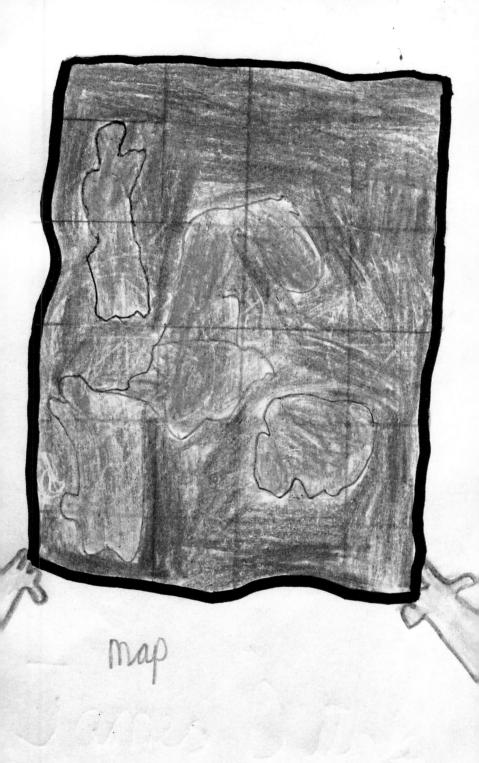

map

of great note, and in Prince's Street possesses the world's most beautiful Street.

Hard, small snowballs, the size of a chemical pill in the bully storm of the air, hit my face bitterly when I was pedalling down the long slope to Greenlaw *via* Carfraemill Inn which I had found to be a shorter way of reaching Greenlaw from Carfraemill Inn than through Lauder.

Showers were clearing off when I was pedalling down the refreshing plain to Coldstream from Greenlaw. I breathed a perfumatory, natural smell of fir trees, grass, in the rainless coolness of the air. The sky was still dull with black clouds. I then visited Coldstream, on the border. It was the chief passage for the English and Scottish armies on the Tweed in former days. I passed Cornhill on the English zone on my way to Wooler.

Owing to the rain, I accepted a very kind invitation by a stout-hearted farmer to stay overnight in a lovely British farm-house near Morpeth, instead of in my tent. He described himself as an English Presbyterian by religion and of Welsh descent. He was brought up in an English home because his Welsh father had married an English wife.

A homely conversation continued between him, his pretty wife, their young daughters and myself at the fire-side in the kitchen. After tea he showed me up stairs to the bedroom, where I slept peacefully.

*　　*　　*　　*

MAY 11. I arrived in the county of Huntingdon from the neighbouring English counties for three days.

York is a very ancient city, where Hadrian, Severus, Constantine and other Roman emperors sometimes

perfumatory, natural

resided. Modern York is beautiful with its bungalows and streets. Oliver Cromwell, Lord Protector of England, was born in Huntingdon, in 1599. He wrote in one of his remarkable letters: "Thus it hath pleased God to give into your hands this other mercy, for which, as for all, we pray God may have all the glory. Indeed your instruments are poor and weak, and can do nothing but through believing and that is the gift of God also." He was a great Christian man, who stood firm in the dark days of warmongers.

Martin Luther, a great German Christian Reformer, also stood steadfastly against the wicked ungodly in Central Europe a few centuries ago. This is one of my favourite biographies.

*   *   *   *

MAY 12. I left here for Dover, *via* Royston, Huntingdon, Ware, London, Writham Heath, Maidstone, Lenham and Canterbury. London is almost situated in the same latitude with Antwerp in Belgium, Leipzig in Germany, Bristol in England and Cork in Eire.

On my arrival in Dover, I missed a steamer at the western docks in the afternoon. The pilot informed me that I might call here to catch a steamer for Calais at 1 p.m. tomorrow. I had covered 666 miles from Cairnbulg.

The French cliffs may be seen from the summit of the Dover cliffs, where I sojourned overnight in my tent above the mighty docks. I noticed that two white clothed cargoes were passing the Straits of Dover far off the docks. I photographed the docks and the sectional cliff with its sloping footpath.

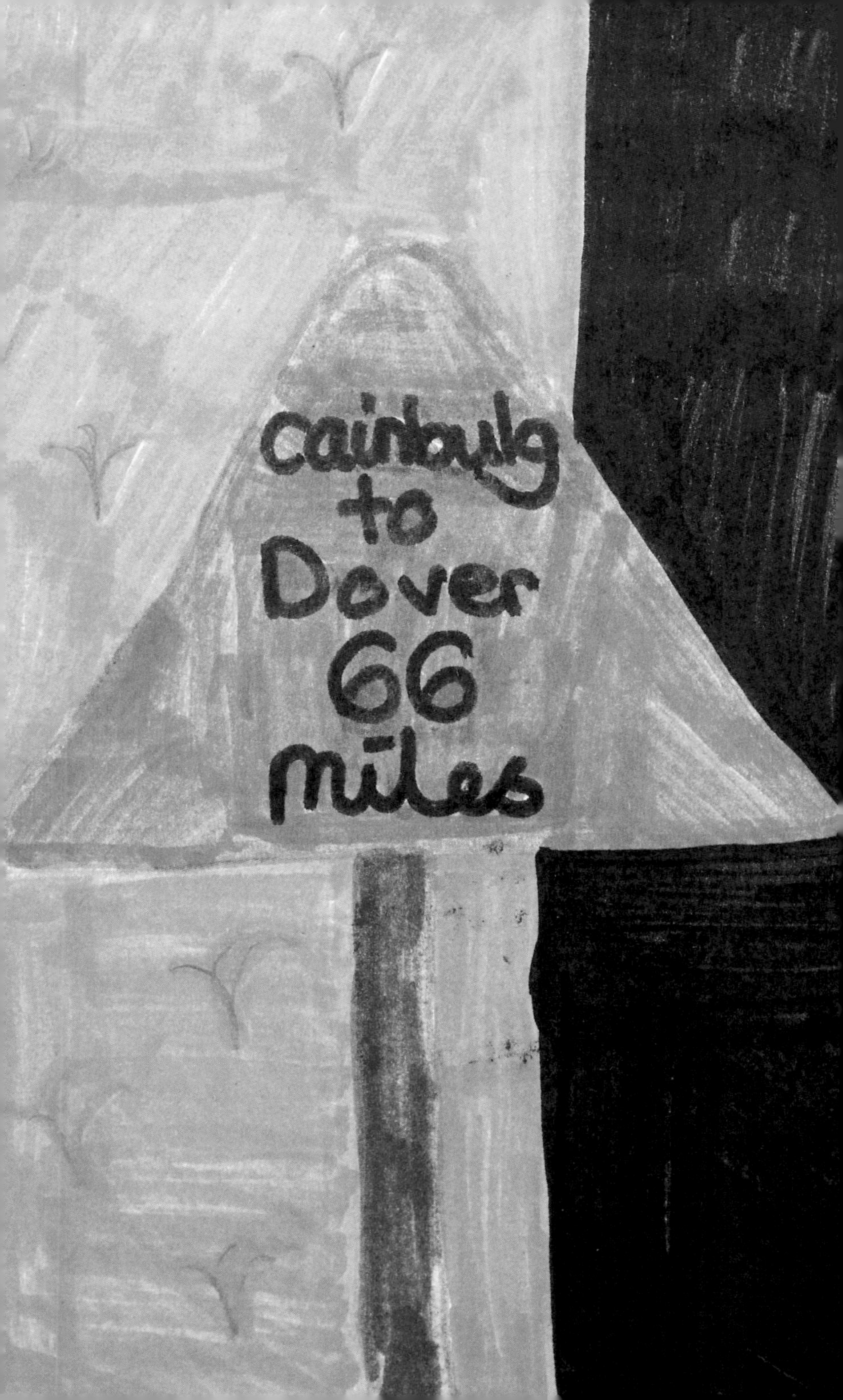
cainbulg
to
Dover
66
miles

MAY 13. At Dover I visited some war ruins beside the beach.

I returned to the western docks where I spoke to an English gentleman. Friendliness grew firmer between us. He accompanied me to the steamer when our British passports were examined.

At 1 p.m. the steamer departed for Calais across the Straits of Dover. After a shave and wash I happened to meet a Scottish hiker in Gordon's tartan kilt. He asked, "Are you a deaf and dumb Cairnbulg man, who is intending a great travel of encouragement to Morocco?" "Yes," I replied, "but how did you know me?" He replied that he had heard about me in the "Buchan Observer," the well-known Peterhead weekly newspaper. I laughingly said to him, "I am amazed to hear what you say. My name has been mentioned in different papers in England too for an English gentleman has sought me."

"Will you please go in and hurry upstairs to join me in the dining room for dinner," he said. "Yes," I replied.

We had a first-class dinner.

"You and I shall travel by bikes to Le Touquet from Calais. We shall stay at the Youth Hostel for one night."

"No," I replied, "I haven't got enough time to do what you ask. I must do my duty in going straight to Southern France."

We arrived on a steamer at Calais, where we were asked to show French custom officers our British, American, French passports for examination at the French Passport Control. A Scots hiker snapped me on the platform at the railway station opposite a steamer. Again one of the English hikers snapped me in the same way. I greeted them and wished them best wishes for their happiness and joy in their hiking tour which may take them to one or other town or village in Belgium. They were hiking to Dunkirk. I gave them a farewell salute when I passed them. They carried heavy rucksacks on their backs.

I met and chatted with an English gentleman at the French train. I shook hands with him a few minutes before his departure for Paris.

I didn't need to study my year-old motor map of France because I remembered the same expedition before. I toured Montreuil and Boulogne last year. I should be able to visit old French towns again to-day.

* * * *

MAY 14. I woke up to a dull morning. My departure for Houden *via* Abbeville, Poix, Beauvais and Mantes. At Poix I saw a number of French brick layers building new houses for the French inhabitants in the valley. I think the French architectural construction is the best class of construction. I climbed to the high and long slope, where I made an appointment with a French saddler. He does an old-fashioned job for his living.

While passing Houden I sought and found a field, where I spent one night. Chartres is an historical place.

* * * *

MAY 15. I contemplated cycling to Montbazon *via* Chartres, Vendome, Tours, where I pitched my tent. At Chartres I visited some historic parts of this French town. It is on the left bank of the Eure, on a hill crowned by its famous cathedral, the spires of which are a landmark on the plain of Beauce, "the granary of France".

The Eure, which divides into three branches, is crossed

23

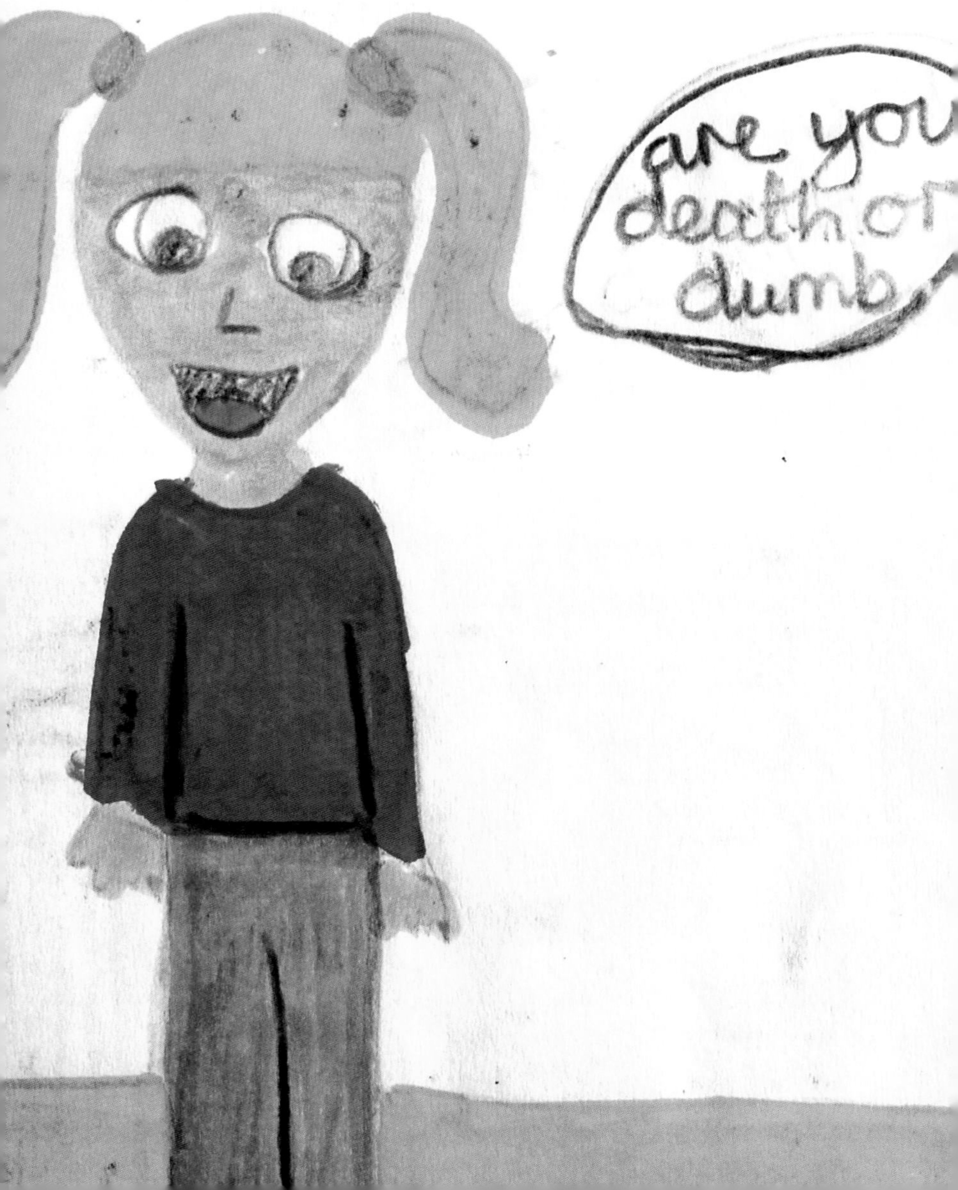
are you death or dumb

by several bridges, some ancient, and is fringed by remains of fortifications, notably the Porte Gaullaume (14th century), flanked by towers.

My departure from Tours was *via* Vendome. I enjoyed being in Tours, which is one of the most beautiful in Western France. I entered the giant entrance that is covered with beautiful decorations, flowers and flags in the centre of the town. There is a magnificent, richly designed bridge beyond the cathedral. Of course it is true that a lovely picture may be seen in the distance of the slope above the Loire. There are silk factories and important printing works, steel works, iron and tin founderies and factories for automobiles, machinery, oil, cement, stained-glass, boots and shoes, porcelain and other goods. A considerable trade is carried on in wine making and in brandy, dried fruits and confectionery.

The weather had been dull and sunlessly warm all day to-day. I left for Montbazon.

* * * *

MAY 16. I cooked food for my breakfast. After breakfast I made a perigrination by cycle to Mansle *via* Chatellevault, Poitiers and Ruffec.

At Chatellevault I wrote and posted numerous postcards on white and black illustrations of towns to my Scottish friends who dwell in the north-east of Scotland. I bought a pocket mirror at the French tobacconist's shop. Branches of the tall trees waved above the traffic. Its brown pillars stand straight. I saw the headstone in which the memorial tribute to Jeanne d'Arc is written between the dyke and street. A busy throughfare is only about three-quarters of a yard from Joan's headstone. I think it is really ugly

for a more healthier way of life ➚

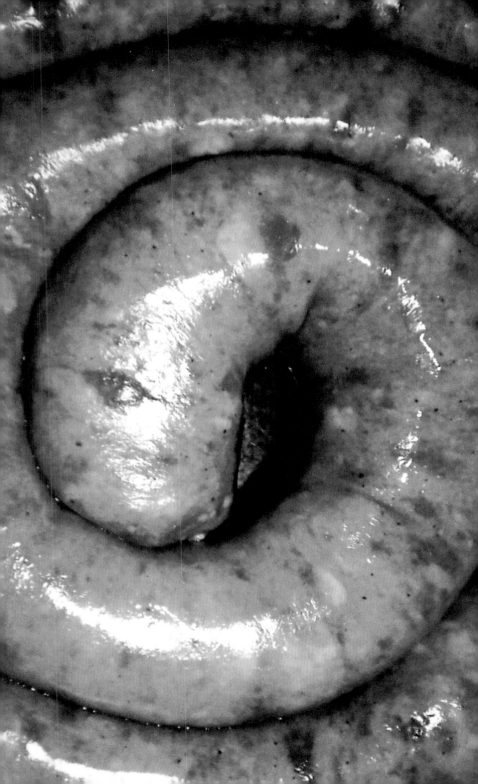

indeed to visit that place, but that is how it was constructed. Of course, I believe millions of French are proud of their own world-famous lady warrior — Joan of Arc. I still remember that I used to read a biographical story about her at the elementary school. I began to measure and conceive the picture of Joan's headstone through one of the camera's two glasses while I had the chance.

The picturesque beauty of Mansle lies in its humble and peaceful river in which the bridge, houses, streets and banks are reflected. I passed Mansle to the countryside main road in the direction of Augouleme for Bordeaux, where I found the inner tube plainly punctured in the back wheel of my bicycle.

I bluntly applied to a young French housemaid for permission to clear the ground round the stable at the side of a big farmhouse for my use, because it is dangerous to mend an inner tube in the traffic. The housemaid kindly permitted me to enter the ground, where I repaired the inner tube at dusk.

A tall and charming farm servant arrived home after spending a good time in angling. He gave a nod and a smile, and taking a few big greyish, pale green snails out of his rucksack, he put them into a wired basket on the ground. They had been accompanied by fish during his run home. It is understood that a farm servant may collect snails until a basket is filled with them for his parents' dinner.

The weather had been mostly raining all day.

* * * *

MAY 17. A screw started to move at the centre of the back wheel after cycling steadily for nearly an hour past.

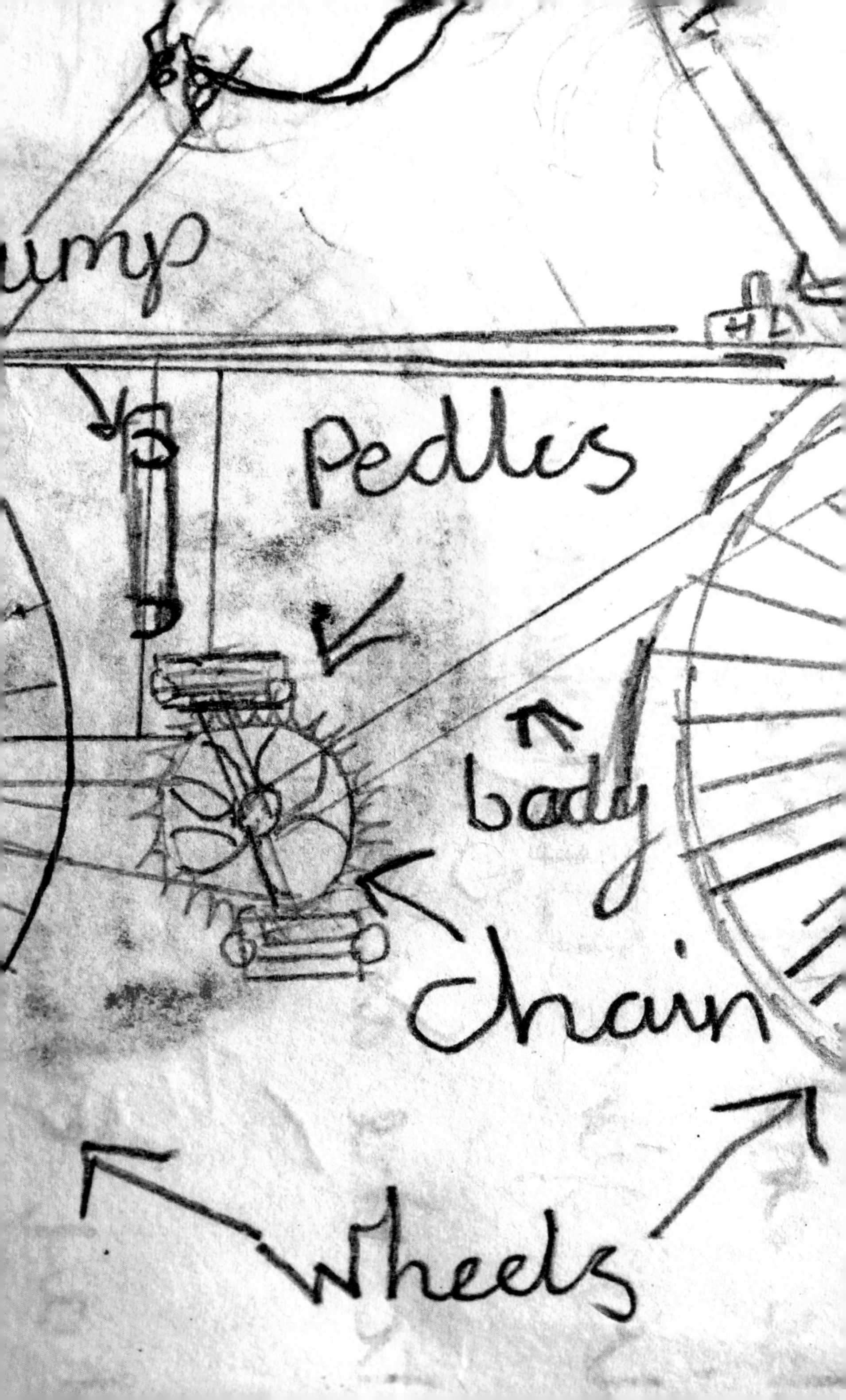

ump

pedles

body

chain

wheels

I attempted to fix the same kind of screw firmly and strongly, but it still remained unsatisfactory. It was of a poor quality material.

At Charente I went to see a French cycle repairer to see if he could sell me a new screw. He said that he had none like mine to sell. He eyed an old French made screw thoughtfully but there was nothing like a British-made screw in this district, so he fixed a French screw at the centre of the back wheel.

I left here for Augouleme, where I happened to find the French screw faulty again. I was going straight to Spain for Morocco and was deeply disappointed as I lost a great deal of time. The journey took me about three miles back to Charente by foot. There I met a French cycle repairer. He said that he could not do that job, so I screwed my own old screw back. I thought my bicycle seemed to be fairly fortified.

I went on my way to La Boutique de le Boulanger (the baker's small shop). A charming young woman with colourful blue eyes sold me a French long loaf for the equivalent of 35 francs (about sixpence in English money). I chatted to her amicably. Her brother invited me to enter the drawing room, where I drank a glass of wine, accompanying his parents. I was delighted to be their guest. For nearly an hour we engaged in homely conversation, then I shook hands with them and said "good-bye," giving them a farewell salute.

I set out for Mansle where I went to see a French cycle dealer. I asked him for a new tyre for the back wheel of my bicycle. A standard charge is 495 francs (about ten shillings in English money) for a French-manufactured tyre and his work together. It is of poor quality material time in France

try, so excited with

and scared on

according to British cyclists, but I bought it because it was better than nothing. I arranged to leave there for Les Nimins, where another French cycle dealer sold me a new tyre at the same price for the front wheel of my bicycle, and also mended a punctured tube very carefully.

I reached Les Nimins where a French cycle dealer did a good job in the dusk. He diverted the attention of his audience of gossiping spectators with his tales of imagination and fun, and finally invited me to sleep under his roof for one night.

*   *   *   *

MAY 18. I made arrangements to pay a visit to the Regional Institution of the Deaf and Dumb (Institution Regionale des Sourds-Mucts) at Poitiers. I reached there. A silvery-white bearded old French man in the person of a director met me. He differentiated words by lip-reading. I did not quite understand him. He had been loyal and faithful to this service for about thirty years. He showed me numerous deaf and dumb pupils and their priests who wore black robes. The director invited me to visit two blind children sitting down reading braille with their touching fingers. I felt sympathetically sorry for them, but they gave the director a smile when he in formed them that I was a Scotsman. I doubt they must have the spirit of real happiness. The blind are able to make the best of life above many and many multitudes with their open eyes. The Lord bless the blind. The director said that the blind pupils are specially granted the best class of education, and they may easily be able to learn, understand and remember geography, arithmetic, religion, history and maps, etc., by the help of braille.

After he had finished an informative chat with me, he showed me the workshop, where I visited a few blind, deaf and dumb employees. They are kindly employed to make loom chairs, baskets, etc. He informed me that a middle-aged, blind, deaf mute comes from Nice. At another bigger workshop, I was shown a pair of new sandals which a tall, deaf and dumb pupil had made well. His other fellow pupils are learning to succeed as shoe repairers, shoemakers, joiners, tailors and gardeners in different classes. An Italian-born pupil displayed to me a wooden bar of lovely design. He is an intelligent wood carver. Most of them are making good jobs. There is a big garden at the back of this building. I left Poitiers for Tours.

At dusk I sought a good field, where I pitched my tent for one night.

*   *   *   *

MAY 19. I was ready to set out to Chartres, where I turned my way which may take me to Ablis for Paris. It began to rain heavily beneath many black clouds, but stopped later, and as the black clouds swept away it became brighter and sunnier. At Ablis I went to a modern grocer's shop to buy a jar of jam, a loaf, and a few tinned foods, which were very expensive.

*   *   *   *

MAY 20. A number of big calves disturbed me from sleeping in my bed bag when they harmlessly pushed my tent with their foreheads. Last night there was no calf to be seen in this field. I hurried to pack up all my belongings while breakfasting because a number of calves would, out of interest, like to play with anything left which belonged

34

to me. I got clear of playing calves. I went, however, on my way to Pans *via* Limours that sunny morning.

After my visit to the gay city of Paris I intended to be going back to the North, but I happened to find an old French engineer at his small engineering workshop in Gonesse that stands about five miles off Paris. I asked him to make a new screw and handed him my old British-made screw to measure and copy. He charged me sixpence for a new screw. It is well screwed at the back wheel of my bike. I feel it may last a long run on a long route. I decided to change to a new route which would take me to Belgium, and then on to Holland.

It was a shock for me to see a great crowd of Parisian car drivers coming home from a quiet northern country. A great queue of cars which must have been about two miles in length. French police, on traffic duty were nearly swept off their feet. Their job was similar to that of the Glasgow police guarding a great crowd of excited football spectators at Hampden in Scotland.

I passed Louvres from Gonesse to a quiet country where I pitched my tent that night.

*   *   *   *

MAY 21. I paid a visit to Senlis before going straight to Cambrai, where I saw a tall French monk who wore a brown robe and a black beard. Senlis can be traced back to the Gallo-Roman township of the Silvanectes which afterwards became Augustomogus. It lies in a valley in the midst of three great forests of Hallatte, Chantilly and Ermenonville. At Cambrai there are numerous French builders constructing a new cathedral in a French type of modern architecture. I felt that it might be a remarkable

May 18th 1951

I made arrangements to pay a visit to the Regional Institution of the Deaf and Dumb at Poitiers in France! I met a man with a white-grey beard.

James Duthie
The Eiffel Tower

My poor drawings

acknowledgement for a would-be tourist to visit a cathedral before it was open to the public. There are numerous French builders constructing new houses for the French people on the other side of the town in the west.

Modern shops are lovely and picturesquely set below a cathedral. The weather is still warm and sunny.

I left Cambrai for Valenciennes *via* Iwuy. At Valenciennes, which is said to owe its name and foundation to one of the three Roman emperors named Valencinian, there is a tramcar service to Quievrain.

In Paris the story is told of the arrival of M. Montelerg. He was a deaf man who was captured by the Germans at Valenciennes during the First World War. He told how, on refusing to work for the Germans he was tied up to a scaffold and whipped for two hours. He succeeded in making his escape to Switzerland, and, after being kindly outfitted by the deaf of Geneva, made his way back into France.

This sunny evening I reached Quievrain situated on the French-Belgium border, from Valenciennes and stayed overnight.

*   *   *   *

MAY 22. A French policeman asked me for my British passport and my British-made bicycle for examination, and permitted me to enter Belgian soil. A Belgian policeman directed me to the bank for money exchange when he finished examining my passport and bicycle. A Belgian policeman's helmet looks something like a Polish general's helmet.

I went upstairs to a confectioner's shop opposite the

bank and bought a thick and big chocolate bar for the price of threepence. I couldn't believe that it only cost threepence. It is as sweet as Britain's famous Cadbury milk chocolate. Its size is about 4 ins. x 8 ins. x ½ in. I myself am very fond of sweets. I could buy plenty of sweets if I wanted in Belgium. No points were necessary at all.

I departed for Brussels *via* Mons, Soignies and Hal from Quievrain. I arrived in Bruxelles (Brussels). A white-helmeted Belgian policeman befriended me by conversation. I asked him to show me a real gun and bullets and he showed it me very carefully. He told me that the police administration is still strong in this city, but no criminal riot nor civil war has been raised here for a very long time as the Brusselian citizens are naturally friendly and responsible in other ways. This Belgian capital shows no enmity, only friendship and peace. A policeman gave me an American lemonade and I drank it sweetly.

At Brussels I happened to receive a kind and hearty invitation to stay in the institution for the deaf and dumb for one night. A headmaster and I had a long knowledge-able talk together. He can speak Flemish, French, English and German fluently, but Flemish is his native tongue. He must, I think, be a man of genius. He showed me round this large and tall building, directing me to a number of classrooms, bathrooms, bedrooms, kitchen, dining room, workshop, gymnasium, etc. They were very clean, well painted and shiningly modern. The pupils were given simple lessons on how to feed two pigs at the small shed, and also other lessons on how to dig a big garden. Two pigs were fat and well fed. A garden was completely filled with flowers, vegetables, fruit trees and hedges.

At suppertime I had two cups of coffee, numerous

buttered slices, fried eggs and potatoes before going straight to my bed. Sleep made me feel at peace in a very comfortable bed behind the giant fireplace of the Old English type in a private bedroom which is strictly reserved for a visitor.

* * * *

MAY 23. I got out of bed this dull morning. I went to the toilet, where I shaved off my beard and washed my face and my hands. In the kitchen I sat down and had a good breakfast with a few young female cooks. So farewell to this Institution. After breakfast I went out to see something of this Belgian capital, visiting the House of Parliament, the King's Palace, different museums, etc. I saw a Belgian warrior in khaki uniform marching past the King's Palace, guarding the Royal Family. I went to buy the Michelin's specially surveyed motor map of Belgium and Holland.

I left Brussels for Ghent *via* Aalst. The Brussels Ghent road is very good and flat for cycling on. It is a warm and sunny day.

I arrived in Ghent. I paid a visit to the institution for the deaf and dumb. A charming director greeted me heartily and made me very welcome to see my old priest Penpal. We had a friendly chat together. The other priests were delighted to meet me and began to talk in a friendly and homely manner. They gave me nods and smiles, and invited me to visit Belgian pupils. I gave a cheer in acknowledgement of cheering pupils, who questioned me about my travels of the past and future and I answered what they wanted to know. They interpreted their national

signs to me. They played football on the cemented pitch and I enjoyed seeing a good match between boys. I am still here. I am intending to go upstairs to my bed.

* * * *

MAY 24. I, in imagination, felt like a feather when I cycled smoothly on a perfectly flat main road which led to Antwerp from Ghent in the direction of St. Nicholas. The scenery was deeply colourful and lovely.

I was unaware that I must bring my cycle with me to the station at the river of Schelde, as the first electric stairs might take me with my cycle down to the deep tunnel and let me go on a walk with my cycle beneath the river to the second electric stairs when I reached Antwerp.

The second electric stairs took me with my cycle up to another station in the city. The width of the River Schelde is as large as the River Thames in London, and there is no charge to enter the tunnel.

Some Belgian people told me that the city was a place of snobs. It is my own idea that Antwerp could be known as the "Edinburgh of the South."

I attended the British Consulate where I had a personal interview with the Consul, who gave me some information, then sent his chaffeur to drive me to the station where I caught a train for Brussels. My bike was then safely left at the British Consulate. I reached Brussels in 30 minutes, then drove through the busy heart of this Belgian capital to the Allied Military Headquarters, where I applied to a British born passport official for permission to enter the British zone, the north-west of Germany, for Denmark. He replied that this office was closed down at the moment. Alas I was disappointed.

A Belgian chauffeur drove me back to the station. He charged me £1 by counting a length of route. Again he forced me to pay him a small tip. I had to wait a few minutes before travelling by train to Antwerp.

I arrived in Antwerp. I went on my way back to the British Consulate, and got my bike back before going to the northern border for the Nederlands.

I went to Wernhout which is situated on the Belgian-Dutch frontier. A Belgian policeman permitted me to pass the frontier to meet a Dutch military officer. My British passport was stamped at the Dutch passport control. I prepared my cycling tour which would take me to a quiet country *via* Breda.

At Breda my tyres made a sweet noise when cycling on a good and clean street made of tiny, long redstone bricks.

Breda is a lovely and colourful Dutch town. Every inch of the village is clean and bright both out side and inside. Some roofs, in which purple, red and green tiles are varnished, make a lovely display, as do the houses, in which doors, windows and fences are well-painted. Part of a tall pump is made of brass which is well polished. Dutch inhabitants are neatly dressed. Dutch women are first-class household workers and their gardens are very clean and neat. I think Holland must be the cleanest country in the world, although Switzerland and Sweden are clean countries too.

There is an old Dutch proverb: "God made the sea, but we make the shore." For a thousand years the making of that shore has been the first thought of Holland's industrious people, who are a wise and determined race. Holland is one of the oddest and most interesting countries in the world.

I cycled into the silence of the country. There I pitched my tent beneath the branches of two fir trees beyond the Dutch peasants' home. At dusk I left to take a walk to attend the cafe restaurant, where I purchased a Dutch round loaf for the price of 6d. A Dutch gentleman kindly offered me a cup of Horlicks and I drank it sweetly. It was his wish to befriend me in conversation; later his girlfriend joined us. We enjoyed a good time here. They are very nice mannered young people, and can write English fluently. I love their national customs very much. This cafe restaurant is known as "Krabbebossen." I shook hands with my young friends and went out of the front door to the road, then to my tent, finding all my belongings still safely there.

I fell asleep in a bed-bag. To-day I have seen a number of Dutch farm-servants who wore sabots.

*   *   *   *

MAY 25. I passed a long giant bridge above the River Maas on the way to Dordrecht. This is a slightly foggy morning.

Dordrecht was one of the wealthiest Dutch ports during the Middle Ages. Old gaol houses line the canal. It was founded by Count Dirk the Third of Holland in 1018, becoming a town about 1200. One of the first towns in the Nederlands to embrace the reformed religion and to throw off the yoke of Spain, it was in 172 the meeting-place of the deputies who asserted the independence of the United Provinces. In 1618 and 1610, it was the seat of the synod of Dort.

Dordrecht presents a picturesque appearance with its busy quays and numerous canals and windmills, its quaint streets and curiously gabled houses.

God made the sea,

but we make the shore

In Holland the roads are reserved for lorries, cars, buses and motor bikes, and the paths for cyclists. There is a path between Dordrecht and Rotterdam. It reminded me of the cycling path in the English county of Durham. It is my intention to leave Dordrecht for Rotterdam now.

I arrived in Rotterdam which is one of the world's busiest commerical ports. Here a Dutch gentleman and I went through the tunnel beneath the River Rhine. We cycled together to visit the deaf and dumb pupils at the local school which was partly damaged by German bombs during the Second World War.

We afterwards visited the school there. He took me to the open main road at the tail of Rotterdam, where he left me, and I began to travel to The Hague *via* Delft.

Rotterdam is situated on the estuary of the Maas and the Rhine. Since 1872 this commercial metropolis has had direct access to the North Sea *via* the Nieuwe Waterweg, an 18-mile channel unobstructed by locks or bridges. Much of central Rotterdam suffered destruction when the city was bombed on May 14th, 1940; later on, when the day of liberation drew near, the Germans blew up many of the harbour installations and blocked the fairways with sunken ships. Almost one-third of the total war damage sustained by the Nederlands was within the boundaries of Rotterdam.

I saw many barges in the channel during my run to the Hague. Dutch bargemen make a good living, and are industrious. One of these barges was carrying tons of coal, but the cargoes of each vary considerably.

I reached The Hague, where I saw some views of the city before going to Scheveningen, to seek the German General Consulate.

The Hague is the seat of the Dutch Government which sits in the central part of this 700-year old city. It is known as "the largest village in Europe." H. M. Queen Juliana opens Parliament during a State visit to The Hague. She is well beloved and highly esteemed by her Dutch people.

After my arrival in Scheveningen I applied to the German General Consulate for permission to enter the British zone, north-west of Germany, for Denmark. My British passport has been permissibly licensed with a printed and stamped visa. I was recommended to pay a few Dutch coins for a new visa. It would be worth staying here for a day, but I had no time.

Scheveningen, the seaside suburb of The Hague, combines the attractions of an old-world fishing village and a cosmopolitan holiday resort. It is a lovely place.

I departed for Haarlem *via* Wassehaar, beyond which is a beautiful golf course, one of the best courses in the Nederlands. Waasehaar is a handsome village which is situated in park-like surroundings north of The Hague.

I saw countless tulips when I arrived in Haarlem, where the houses, barges and bridges are beautifully coloured and mirrored in the numerous narrow canals, reflecting light and shade and presenting such a variation of colour as would delight any artist.

Haarlem is a town in the Province of Noord Holland (North Holland). It was a prosperous place in the middle of the 12th century, receiving its first town charter from William the Second, Count of Holland and king of the Romans, in 1245.

In the evening I was ready to go to Amsterdam. Here I was kindly invited to stay in the modern home of my Dutch deaf and dumb friend for one night. I had a long talk with

The nail that sticks out gets pounded

his son and daughter who can speak and hear well. They are good at writing English. Their father is a cabinet-maker by trade. Their mother died a few months ago.

*   *   *   *

MAY 26. Amsterdam, capital of the Netherlands, is known as "The Venice of the North." In this remarkable city — a city whose growth can be traced to the concentric semi-circles of its main canals, like the rings of a tree-trunk — the fascinating mixture of the old and new permits one to pass in a moment from busy streets and up-to-date shops to the peaceful backwater of an ancient "gracht". Along the quays of these typical canals stand proud patrician dwellings built by the Dutch merchant princes of Amsterdam in the 16th and 17th centuries. I passed in a great canal to another quay in about ten minutes by ferry-boat.

I cycled to a picturesque fishing village named Volendam. Here I visited one of the local shops where souvenirs, postcards, etc., were sold. A passing tourist snapped a number of Dutch fishermen with their wrinkled, Rembrandt-like faces, mending nets. They were dressed in old-fashioned garments. They may appeal to the pencil or camera of passing strangers. An old fisherman smiled when he passed me as I sat on a wooden form on the shore. I was amazed to see two young Kentish cyclists behind the shop. There are a number of sailing boats left at the harbour.

Volendam is remarkable for its quaint buildings and the picturesque costume of the villagers, who are of a singularly dark and robust type. It has its origin in the building of the great sea dam for the new water way to Edam in the middle of the 14th century. On the seaward side of the

54

dyke are some houses built on piles in the style of lake dwellings.

I prepared for my journey which will take me to the 21-mile long Zuyder Zee Dyke *via* Hoorn.

In the middle of the great dyke I paid a visit to the modern tower from which I got a wonderful view of the two seas known as "Wadden Zee" and "Yesel meer." I went downstairs to the restaurant from the tower, where I bought and posted a few postcards to my Scottish friends.

I reached Leeuwarden *via* Harlingen and Franeker, where I slept well in the home of my other deaf and dumb friend for one night. He is a cabinet maker by trade. He told me of his experience and work, showing me lovely chairs, drawers, etc., made by himself. He must be a highly skilled tradesman. Congratulations to his excellent works!

Leeuwarden is easily accessible from all parts of the province of Friestland by road, rail and canal.

*   *   *   *

MAY 27. This morning I enjoyed a good breakfast with a cabinet-maker, his wife and son. They accompanied me to the country, where they left me and turned right to a narrow road as they were in tending to visit their own friends at a farm. They wished me farewell. I went on my way to Groningen.

After my arrival in Groningen I met another deaf and dumb cabinet-maker whose German-born wife kindly invited me to a good dinner in their beautiful home. It was a well furnished place with arm chairs, carpets, tables, flowers, etc. He and I went down to the school for the deaf and dumb boys and girls. He told them about my exploratory expedition.

56

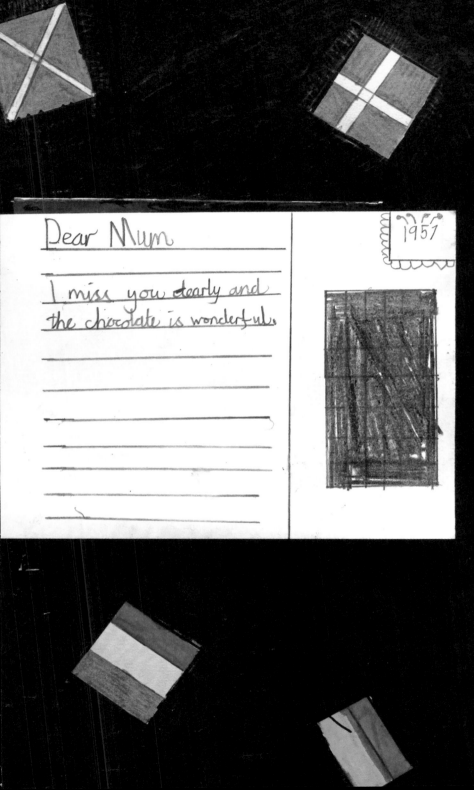

Dear Mum

I miss you dearly and
the chocolate is wonderful.

1951

Groningen is one of the finest cities in Holland, thanks to the well conceived plan on which it is laid out, with two broad squares in the centre on which all the main streets converge.

Unfortunately for Groningen it was the only city in the north of the Nederlands to suffer severe war damage, and that occurred in April, 1945, when the defeated Germans put up a resistance which, though stubborn, was fore-doomed to failure. But the city still possesses many fine old buildings.

I cycled on the canal to Veendam in the direction of Hoogezand, where I met a deaf and dumb fellow. I departed for Nieuwe Schans which is situated on the Dutch-German frontier *via* Winschoten. I received permission to pitch my tent on the right bank of the road between the border entrance and the Dutch passport officers' hut. I slept so peacefully that night.

*　　*　　*　　*

MAY 28. A German policeman stopped and asked for my British passport to be handed to him for examination when I entered German soil. At the British Zone Passport Control an officer passed my passport and gave me some information. I asked a German policeman a question. He laughed and replied that a British tourist may easily be arrested by Russian warriors if he enters the Russian zone (Iron Curtain). I told him that I still intended to continue my cycling tour which might take me to Denmark *via* Hamburg. I shook hands with him and went on my way.

I toured Leer, Oldenburg, Bremen and Rotenburg before reaching the German innkeeper's field near Hamburg, where I spent one night.

How many buttons can YOU count?

I met two young German chimney sweeps whose faces were dirtily black-marked. They wore top-hats. They were coming home to Oldenburg from their work. I thought they looked like playing boys.

A German master baker's middle-aged wife looked me straight in the eyes, and listened to me. She sold me numerous iced cakes which were as sweet as the Scottish iced cakes. I imagine their business must be well thought of in the mind of the public.

*   *   *   *

MAY 29. I passed Hamburg which. is a seaport town in the Prussian province of Hanover, on the left bank of the southern arm of the Elbe.

After my arrival I bought some brownish-black bread at the German baker's shop in Hamburg. I saw many empty, houseless streets and some ruined buildings which were terribly overwhelmed by the Royal Air Force and other Allied airmen during the Second World War. I passed the twin towers of the mighty road bridge above the Elbe to the northern boundary of this industrial, commercial city.

I went ahead to Rendsburg in the direction of Neumunster. The afternoon I described as pale greenish blue with white clouds in fine sunshine.

I saw a Russian motor cargo passing an open bridge after reaching Rendsburg. A Communist flag waved at the stern of the cargo.

Rendsburg is situated on the Kaiser Wilhelm canal which is the safest, most convenient, shortest and cheapest route from the North Sea and the Baltic, increasingly used by merchant vessels. It is known as the Keil Canal.

A German policeman ordered me to go back to the road,

but I took no notice of him. I think he must still be a pro-Nazi sympathiser.

In the early evening I left for Schleswig where I saw numerous white yachts in a beautiful Firth which is an opening surronding the Baltic Sea about twenty-five miles in length. It is a prosperous, picturesque place with its white hotel, streets, houses and trees. I turned right along the road until I came to the forest where I threw sticks away and cleared a pitch for my tent among tall and thin trees about one hundred and twenty yards off the left bank of a Flensburg-Schleswig main road. My tent, in which I slept well, was hidden all night by deep shadows beneath the branches of the trees.

*   *   *   *

MAY 30. I woke up in the morning at sunrise and counted and examined all my belongings after having a good breakfast. I pumped the tyres of my bicycle, went back to the main road which is very good and flat for cycling, and contemplated going to Flensburg.

I saw the well-built aerodrome during my run to Flensburg. It is the Royal Air Force's property.

I started my arrival in Flensburg, which is a growing seaport in the Prussian province of Schleswig Holstein, at the head of the Flensburg Fjord. The town was probably founded in the twelfth century.

I went straight to the German-Danish frontier after a short visit to Flensburg.

A German police official stamped my passport. Another German police official permitted me to enter the Danish border. In Denmark I bought ice cream at a small shop which is attached to the Danish bank at the border.

20/9/51

A German Sweeper

Pg6

/5/51

Pg 7

I reached Aabenraa, which is situated at the head of a bay of that name, being an arm of the little Belt. It has a good harbour and a large carrying trade. It has a lovely fjord between the range of hills. The sun was shining very warm and bright just now.

I left Aabenraa for Hadersley which lies in a valley on the Hadersleben fjord which is about nine miles in length, and communicates with the little Belt.

I travelled by cycle to Vejle *via* Kolding. Here all the streets and buildings reminded me of my one month holiday sojourn in this beautifully situated town in June-July, 1947, when I was coming down the slope to meet my old Danish friend; he greeted me, quickly remenbering me. He has a tailoring business of his own. He employs a deaf and dumb young tailor and a hearing young tailoress. He is a smart business man. He himself is a deaf mute. He has a deaf and dumb wife and a deaf and dumb little daughter.

The town of Vejle occupies a sort of isthmus of solid ground between the fjord. It is an old dwelling place, but its buildings are new owing to many fires. It has many very good model social institutions, hospitals, houses for old age pensioners, for people with large families, nurseries, etc.

It is a factory town. Originally the small rivers, which are very rapid, delivered the motive power to the factories. Now most of them use electricity. The Danish Cotton Spinning Mills are the oldest in Denmark, the air being especially favourable for the threads. Windfield-Hansens Spinning Mills, textile and weaving Mills, a large soap factory (Worning and Petersen) who formerly exported soap to England and India, etc. It has several factories for baking powder, spices, leather, stoves, and so on.

Vejlian inhabitants laugh at a passing tourist in a street when they see a towel or book or news paper, or bag of biscuits in his arms. They must put food or anything into their shopping bags first before going out of their homes to do shopping or their friend's party. College students must carry books in their book-bags when they go to the college. This is a very funny and strange custom. I think it is a lot of nonsense and rubbish,

I resided in the home of Herr Svend G. Leerager in Havnegade in the neighbourhood of Vejle's commercial docks for one night. His wife, Frau Esther Leerager, belongs to Bornholm.

*   *   *   *

MAY 31. At Vejle I went on my way to visit my old Danish friends Herr and Frau Kronhoff whose home residence is in Dalgrade in the neighbourhood of the wood at the slope. They are Christian believers in the word of God and are steadfast Protestants. They were very pleased to make me welcome when I arrived in their old Danish house. I was surprised indeed to see my oil portrait of a horse and its foal hanging up at the window-place in a big lounge room. Afterwards I had a good time with them. I went on my way to visit their married daughter — Frau Esther Simonsen — who dwells with her husband and family in Staldgardsgrade.

There are many merchants' surnames painted or engraved in the bars of their shops and many called "Hansen," a common surname in Denmark. That is why Herr and Frau Hansen became Herr and Frau Kronhoff, in accordance with their deaf and dumb son's own wish,

It is better to dwell in the wilderness,

than with a contentious
and an angry woman

through the Copenhagen registrar. The change of surname cost a good bit of money.

Mirrors are hung in the middle of every front window of the red-tiled roofed houses, so that Danish householders see the picture of passers-by at the window without having to open the windows and look on people.

A Danish cycle repairer mended a few wires of my rear cycle wheel. He charged me two kroners (about two shillings in English money).

I left Vejle for Nybord *via* Middelfart and Odense. It was hard work cycling on a high, hilly main road to Odense from Middelfart. Lovely views of Odense are worth seeing.

At Nyborg I caught a boat which took me across the Store Belt to Korsor. Electric train and carriages were carried into the boat. They had· just been returning home from Hamburg and Rome.

Nyborg is situated in one of the Danish Isles named Funen. It is a prosperous place with a seaport and yachts.

I left Korsor by ferry-boat and travelled towards Soro *via* Slagelse.

I was kindly granted permission to pitch my tent at the corner of a field against the garage for one night after passing Soro. I acknowledged a Danish garage proprietor's smile for me and I chatted to him in a friendly mood. Denmark has a smile for everybody who likes to see a smile, just as some other countries shout with laughter or look sad or even positively gloomy.

June, 1951

JUNE 1. I breakfasted on tea and biscuits, then went on my way to see the Roskilde Cathedral which was begun in 1170 by Bishop Absalon, the founder of Copenhagen. It is known as the "Westminster Abbey" of Denmark. The olden Christian monarchs and practically the whole line of Oldenborg were buried in this church. The blue waters of Roskilde Fjord are very easy to look at in Roskilade but I did not have time to visit the fjord.

The weather was foggy and wet, turning sunny later during my run to Roskilde in the direction of Ringsted. Roskilde lay on my route to Copenhagen. The sun was shining on my face.

At Copenhagen I intended to pay a visit to the home of my old deaf and dumb friend in the forenoon but he was at work so his neighbour told me to come back to meet him at 4 o'clock.

At Christiansborg (the House of Parliament) I saw a leading Danish M.P. who gave a noble political speech in audience of other members in the House of Commons. I looked down on members from the gallery. I passed royal photographs in which King Frederik the Ninth and his Swedish-born Queen Consort paid a State visit to Christiansborg when I went downstairs to the exit door.

I went on my way to the Amalienburg Palace where the Royal Life Guards are on duty and every day they march through the great square. They are grand fellows, these gentlemen and guardsmen, in their light-blue trousers and their dark-blue coats glistening with polished buttons and crossed with white breast-straps. Enormous black busbies gave them a top-heavy look and caused them to perspire

70

freely. The lieutenants, who must have graduated from military college in their early teens, peered out like babes from underneath this martial millinery. The Royal Life Guard frankly invited me to snap him behind the great entrance. It was an opportunity to snap the wonderful statue of King Frederik the Fifth seated on his enormous bronze horse in the middle of the square. I gave my camera to a nice looking Danish constable, who snapped me at the statue of King Frederik the Fifth.

There was no Royal Standard at the mast on King Frederik's palace residence because he was away from home on a pleasure trip or a State visit. He is very fond of motoring and yachting. He is a very enthusiastic sportsman. He is descended from King Gorm the Gamle, who had reigned in the kingdom of Denmark from 900 to 940 A.D., and is in the fifty-first genealogical line to King Gorm the Gamle.

Two horses-draw a cart and only carry a light burden; they are well looked after because their own flesh will be the future national meat for the Danes. Some Danish people think it may make poor meat if the horses have been made to work too hard. I myself do not like to eat this meat; it is harder meat than cow meat.

I visited the Danish deaf mute, old age pensioners at the Institute for the Deaf. They are very fortunate and pay no rent. They are nice people, these gentlemen and ladies, wearing plain garments. One fat Dane started to light and smoke a cigar when going to town shopping.

I signed my name in a visitors' book, in accordance with the president's wish.

After 4 o'clock I returned to Denmarksgade (Denmark Street), where I went upstairs to knock at the front door of

my old deaf and dumb friend's house, and he greeted me. I was kindly invited to stay in his home for three days.

My bicycle is locked in the shed at the back of my friend's house. Most Copenhagen citizens are a cycle minded race. Most of them are in the habit of borrowing other people's bikes. Old, young, tall, small, rich and poor, they are all on bicycles. It is not wise to pretend that an American or Scottish tourist believes the common joke that he can just pick up a bicycle in the street and put it down again when he is tired of riding it. Bicycles, contrary to the impression travellers may inadvertently acquire, are not the property of the State, but are privately owned.

I dined on mince, mashed potatoes, custard pudding, jelly, coffee and biscuits with my friend and his deaf and dumb wife.

We called on our old tall Danish friend and his hearing wife tonight. I used to go down to the fish market where he cures fish, in Fredericia four years ago. He is a jolly fellow, this grand fishworker.

*   *   *   *

JUNE 2. Politiken is Denmark's greatest national newspaper. A tall and stout editor of over six feet asked me numerous questions and I answered them. He wanted me to be given a cup of tea and biscuits in his office. He eventually ordered his photographer to bring a marvellous first-class camera to him, and I was photographed. An article about me may be published in *Politiken* on Monday morning.

I wanted to see some views of Copenhagen before dinner-time as I was going for a dinner party with my

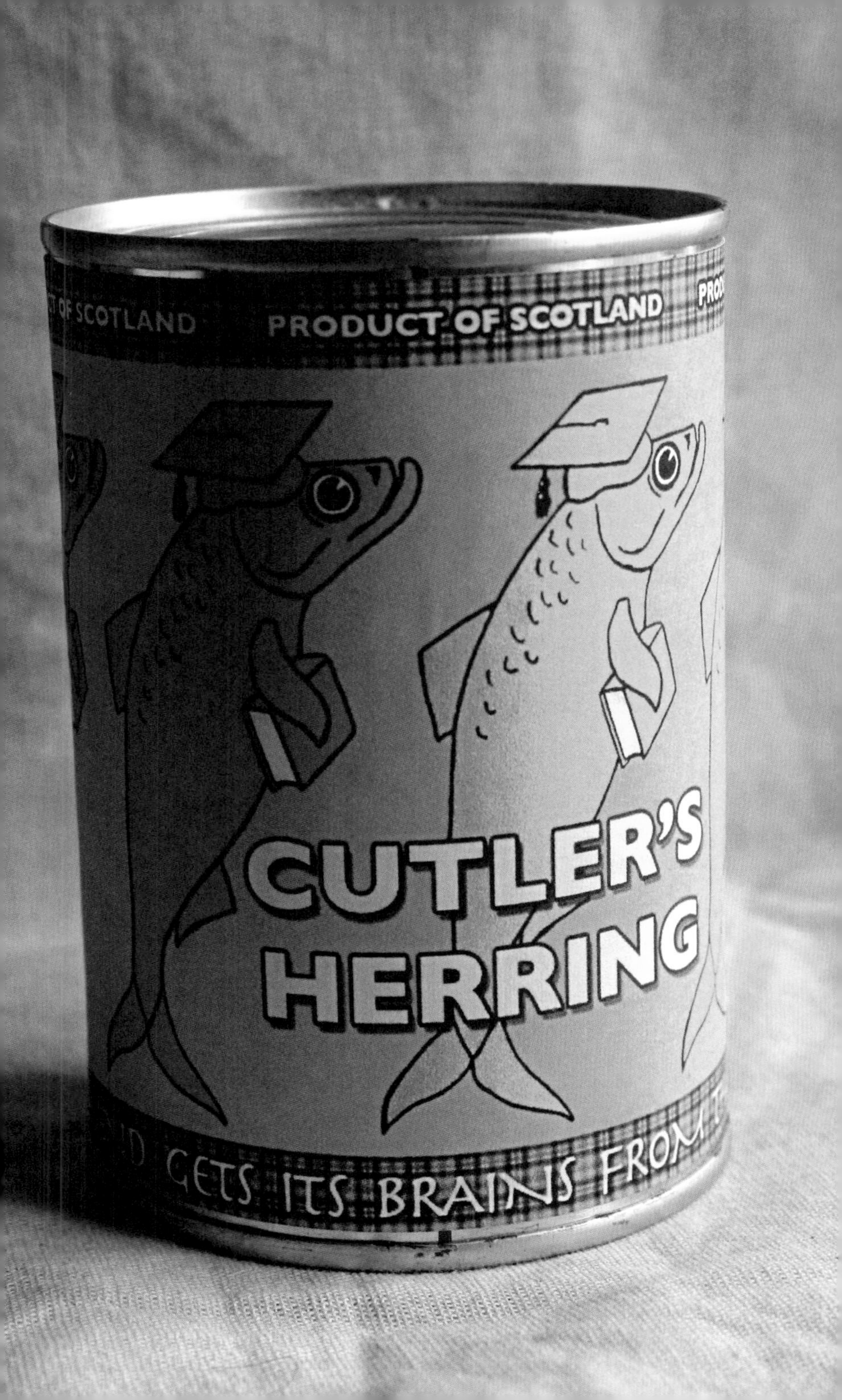
PRODUCT OF SCOTLAND
CUTLER'S
HERRING
GETS ITS BRAINS FROM

friends in Denmark Street. My friend, his wife and I went out to call at the deaf and dumb club in the evening.

It was a sunny afternoon. l talked with two deaf and dumb young Norwegian men who are spending their summer holiday in Copenhagen. It was a little difficult in comprehending what they meant in queer Norwegian signs.

I enjoyed drinking a cup of coffee and eating biscuits with friends in another home of a Swedish born wife and her Danish husband who are both deaf mutes. We went on our way to Denmark Street to sleep.

The Danes and Swedes, in conversation, spell with one hand. The Swedish alphabetical letters of I, M and N are related to the Danish sign language for the deaf and dumb, otherwise the Swedish sign language differs from the Danish sign language. A Dane may easily understand how to become a successful one-handed speller in Swedish signs when he meets a Swedish blonde in Sweden. Swedes and Danes can understand one another as Americans and English understand one another. Dovstum skotte in Swedish means Dovstum skotsk (Scottish deaf mute) in Danish. A Swede does not need to translate a long sentence or paragraph or composition when he reads the Danish daily newspaper. I have never attempted transla-tion when I read a book on Scandinavian travels written by a well known American author. Savior or traveler in American means Saviour or traveller in English.

*　*　*　*

JUNE 3. I fed numerous pigeons in the Town Hall square which is in the centre of the city. It is a warm and sunny morning to-day.

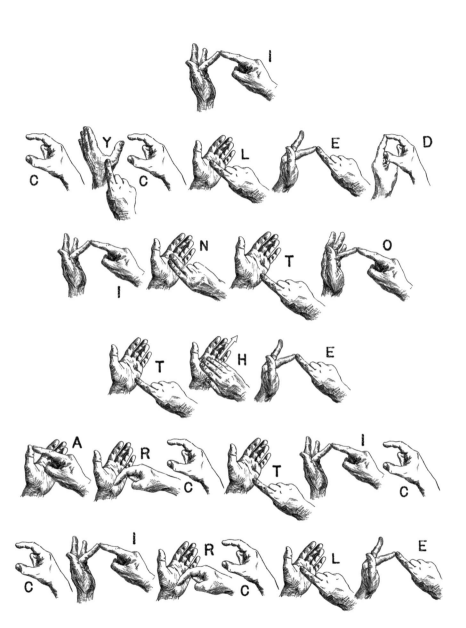

My old friend pointed out to me the Round Tower which stands in the centre of Old Copenhagen and was built by King Chrition the Fourth in 1642. The present Danish monarch is the fourteenth descendant of King Christian who died in 1648. A Danish postage stamp bearing a purple-coloured picture of the Round Tower celebrated the three-hundredth anniversary of his reign in 1942.

We travelled by tramcar to Soberg, where we were invited to have a grand dinner party with his well beloved aunt, her husband and family. I dined at the long table with her eldest son who had just come home from Greenland. After dinner he talked of his whale-hunting experience. He wears a Danish naval uniform, and is a skilled and good seaman. His mother is a good-hearted friend of highly spiritual intentions whom I loved. I felt like a well consoled son when she smilingly conversed with me in amiable compassion. She is a cheerful giver. I shall never forget her Christian example. She is a good wife to her husband and also a good mother to her family of ten. She is a Christian Protestant believer in the word of God.

Soberg is one of Copenhagen's northern branches. It is a prosperous and healthy place with council houses and streets and trees.

* * * *

JUNE 4. I got out of bed in the early morning as my old friend had to begin work. After breakfast I shook hands with him and said good-bye. I intend to make my way along the coast to Elsinore.

I departed from Copenhagen for Elsinore in the sunny morning. At Bellevue, which is Copenhagen's favourite place for excursions, I saw a lovely bathing beach.

I finally reached Elsinore, where I caught a ferry boat for Sweden. I saw the Kronborg Castle which was erected by King Frederik the Second in 1585. It lies only thirty miles off Copenhagen. Every year Shakespeare's *Hamlet* is performed in Kronburg Castle courtyard by leading foreign companies.

A Danish passport official asked for my British passport. He handed me my passport back when he finished his examination. I began to cross Helsingborg at Elsinore.

At Helsingborg I passed through to Sweden. Two national flags were still waving at the tail of the pier. A group of English holidaymakers were standing behind the harbour station, they were travelling northwards to visit Stockholm and Trondhelm and Oslo before going back to England.

I carried on to Varnamo *via* Marlaryd and Ljungby. Marlaryd is a market town with wood industries. It is a commercial and industrial town with seven thousand inhabitants. I passed a lovely lake to Varnamo, where a Christian Swede and his loyal comrade helped me to go with them across the river to the park, where the ground was flat and we pitched my tent. They were keenly interested in my cycling explorations.

Helsingborg is the principal entrance gate for the Continental tourists and business men who enter to go up to the Swedish Capital or Arctic Circle.

I found three young Swedish cyclists resting on the dyke at the brae, so I took a rest for a while and we soon became firm friends. They told me that they will be able to cycle down to Malmo which is Sweden's most southerly city. They are on holiday at the moment. I wished them best wishes for their future happiness and a good journey.

Map
of
Sweden
(inside)

*   *   *   *

JUNE 5. I found my priceless motor map of Sweden was missing from my tent when I finished my breakfast, but I remembered that one of the Swedes had put it into one of his jacket pockets while chatting last night. Alas! he was absent-minded; he was no thief.

At Varnamo I left my bike at the cafe restaurant, where I carefully listed the names of towns which I may visit before reaching Stockholm. Varnamo is a beautiful dwelling place on the River Lagan and Lake Vidostern, and is also an industrial dwelling place with furniture, rubber, yarn and rail factories. The local residents are mostly employed in various factories.

I went northwards on my run to Jonkoping *via* Skillingaryd and Vaggeryd. Jonkoping is on the southern tip of Lake Vattern and is famous for its match factory which is well known all the world over. The eastern neighbourhood of Jonkoping is Huskvarna.

I continued along the eastern shore of Lake Vattern, following the main road which claims to be the most beautiful road in Sweden.

Lake Vattern is the second largest lake in Sweden and the fourth largest in Europe. It is more than 100 miles in length and nearly fifty miles in breadth, and is very beautiful. It is fairly deep too, in places reaching a depth of four hundred and twenty-seven feet, and the water is cold and extremely clear. The surrounding district is rich in historical memories of the past, and there is evidence of its being inhabited in the Stone Age.

A stretch of water changes from the calm mirror of a lake to a dark angry sea.

67   EXT. ROAD, EASTERN SHORE OF LAKE VATTERN — MORNING   67

        DUTHIE is cycling alongside the huge lake in blazing
        sunshine. He passes a group of shirtless LUMBERJACKS high
        up on the wooded slopes. As DUTHIE speeds off up the road,
        the LUMBERJACKS lay down their tools in unison.

                        LUMBERJACK CHORUS
                          (Swedish signs)
                Oh, Beautiful Lake Vattern!
                100 miles long,
                50 miles in breadth.
                Behold! In places
                'Tis 427 feet in depth.

68   EXT. FRASERBURGH HARBOUR — MORNING   68

                        CHORUS OF FISHERMEN
                That's all very well
                But beware the treacherous swell!
                A clear mirror
                Of calm serenity, may
                Without warning
                Become a dark, angry sea.

The woodland is only about three miles north of Huskvarna, and here I took off my shirt owing to the hot climate, copying the sunburnt Swedish lumber jacks who need no shirts to wear during the hard work among the trees. I made my dinner in the wood before proceeding to Granna which lies pleasantly in the middle of the eastern coast of Lake Vattern. Quite near is the Island of Visingso, with its imposing ruins of Visingborg castle, destroyed by fire in 1718, when Russian prisoners of war were interned here. A steamer crosses to the famous island from Granna.

I departed here for Linkoping *via* Odeshog, Mjolby and Viby. At Linkoping I made my way down the footpath to see the ancient cathedral which was dated in 1230. It is one of the most remarkable architectural monuments in Sweden.

A few miles north of Linkoping, I pitched my tent for the night, which was dark and cloudy.

* * * *

JUNE 6. It was cold getting out of my tent on a dull and sunless morning. Afterwards I packed and cycled away to see the Gota canal where there are numerous pleasure steamers and yachts. From Stockholm to Gothenburg there are two great lakes, Vattern and Vanern, extending through four hundred miles of beautiful countryside. The canal, which was built a hundred years ago, cuts through the two ancient Gothic provinces, Vastergotland in the west and Ostergotland in the east, and links the two lakes by a two-way traffic system.

I proceeded to Norrkoping, Sweden's fourth largest city and a most important commercial and industrial town with several fine parks and gardens.

84

Jim was here 05/06/51

Swedish roads are the worst in Europe, and I became bespattered with mud and very dirty.

On arriving in Nykoping I visited the industrial town and many of its buildings. There are buildings which were erected during the Middle Ages. These are residences of several Swedish kings. King Birger Magnusson of the Folkunga dynasty imprisoned his two brothers, Duke Erik and Duke Valdemar in one of the Nykoping castle's towers in 1317 and let them starve to death. The Town Hall was erected in the seventeenth century.

On my way to Sodertalje *via* Vagnharad I saw a nervous-looking badger running across the road in the wild forest.

Sodertalje is a prosperous place with its lovely canal which unites Lake Malaren with the Baltic. I enjoyed my visit to this town.

I pitched my tent on hilly ground at the brae just outside Sodertalje.

*   *   *   *

JUNE 7. Happily I was able to visit Stockholm which is a spiritually democratic and beautiful city on the coast.

Sweden's world-wide architectural fame has witness in the modern construction of the city's imposing office and business buildings; the latest developments in apartments and housing design.

One of the Swedish travel agents' assistants recommended me to call at the Norwegian Legation where I had an interview with two young assistants who offered me a few free booklets on Norwegian Arctic Expeditions. The Norwegian Legation is good enough to help a tourist who contemplates spending his holiday in the western fjords or Trondhjem district or Oslo Fjord.

I went downstairs to the private bathroom where I had a hot bath. I still remember an old motto: "Cleanliness is next to Godliness"!

Dagens Nyheter is Sweden's greatest daily news paper with sixteen pages. It costs about twopence and a halfpenny (20 ore in Swedish money). A neatly dressed Swedish reporter wished me to be photographed for the Dagens Nyheter. Stockholmers are interested in my globe-trotting.

I sat reading booklets in the vicinity of Riddarholm church on the Riddarholm Island across the water. The State church is the resting place of the Swedish kings and is known as the "Westminster Abbey" of Sweden. The late tall and silverhaired King Gustav the Fifth was buried in this church last year. He was a well-beloved king and is greatly missed. He is remembered as a good democratic monarch, and a keen tennis player.

I went up to visit Frau Eisa Fondoltus at the beautifully built council house and saw Lake Malaren and the Town Hall through one of the large windows. I admired them very much. Frau Fondoltus' faith fully continues her spare-time work amongst the deaf and dumb at the club, where her father, now dead, used to be a highly esteemed deaf and dumb missioner. Determination makes her follow her father's footsteps and although she can speak and hear well, she gives sympathetic support to the unfortunate deaf mute whom she particularly admires.

I was kindly given an invitation by Herr Osvald and Frap Alice Dahlgren to stay in their beautifully furnished flat for two and a half days when Frau Fondoltus took me down with her to visit them in the evening. Herr O. Dahlgren is a member of the Swedish Deaf and Dumb Association and also secretary of Stockholm's Deaf and

Dumb Association. He is a capable ambassador. He is a printer by trade and he and his wife are both deaf and dumb.

Herr O. Dahlgren showed me his photograph album. I was greatly interested to read about his holiday with friends in the Swedish Arctic Circle. He said to me: "A Swedish Lapp chipped and stirred reindeer meat in coffee for a drink; he heartily induced me to clear up his hut and let me sleep alone; he guards a flock of reindeer all night."

*　　*　　*　　*

JUNE 8. In Old Stockholm I noticed a few smartly-dressed Finnish holidaymakers with small metal badges pinned in their lapels; these badges are national Finnish flags. A number of ships are officially stationed at the eastern boundary of the Old Town opposite the two islands named Skeppsholmen and Kastellholmen; a Finnish steamer goes on a regular sail across the Gulf of Bothnia to Helsinki, Finland's capital.

I felt some excitement in the warm-growing air on my way to visit the school for the deaf and dumb and my feet became slightly burned. A male teacher asked me to give his pupils an introductory, short lectucre in the classroom, and he began to interpret what I said by means of a blackboard. They were interested in my adventurous enterprise. I said that it may surely sound impossible to attempt to cycle to the North Cape in the northmost Norwegian province of Finnmark. Suddenly he grasped the idea, begging me to abandon my future Arctic explorations; I see he is no person of courage.

Returning to Old Stockholm I visited the Royal Palace (Kongliga Slottet), Stock Exchange (Borsen) and

Parliament House (Riksdagshuset), etc. In one of its narrow and stone-paved streets it was my happiness to see a real photograph of a Swedish hiker at the photographer's studio. He had carried a heavy rucksack with a Swedish flag on his back, touring North Africa. Numerous Royal coats-of-arms can be seen above or below some shops displaying Swedish goods to catch the eye of a customer.

I can say with the late Dr. W. R. Roe: "Someone has written that the people of Sweden hold their heads a little high. Well, she is a country with a grand romantic past, faithful to her old traditions, and yet to the fore in almost every field of modern exploit and enterprise. No country gives more attention than Sweden to its children, who, after all, are the making or marring of a nation, and happily here no difference is made between the deaf and the hearing."

Personally I admire the Swedish way of life with all my heart.

I walked back to the home of Herr O. and Frau A. Dahlgren, where I dined with them in the sunny evening. I always think a Swedish dinner is lighter than a Scotch dinner.

After dinner Herr O. Dahlgren and I travelled by tram-car to visit the deaf and dumb club where he showed me over this reasonably furnished club and introduced other deaf and dumb members to join in a friendly chat with me.

Later Frau Fondultus was delighted to meet me and talk to me. She cleared the table and opened her map of Northern Sweden, carefully explaining to me where to stay in Northern Sweden and offering me very helpful advice. She said to me: "You ought to fill your rucksack with

Oatcake stories ⟶

plenty of food when you are intending your journey to North Cape from Rovaniemi. Rovaniemi is the capital of Finnish Lapland."

Herr O. Dahlgren and I came out to the night cafe where we drank coffee and ate iced cakes with a few deaf mute Swedes before returning home.

*　　*　　*　　*

JUNE 9. I gave Herr O. and Frau Dahlgren a farewell salute. I had promised to visit Frau Fondoltus at the large firm opposite the Central Station this morning, where she is employed as a secretary.

She phoned to a travel agent for some information for me and handed me a token of a Finnish Consul's address. She asked me to go with her to the canteen for breakfast. I shook hands with her, and said to her: "Good-bye to you, my friend."

Attendance was made on a Finnish consul with whom I had an interview.

Beyond Stockholm my bicycle had a puncture. I am preparing to go northwards to Uppsala *via* Marsta, where I had the puncture repaired. The weather has been very sunny but showery later.

On my arrival I took a great delight in visiting Uppsala. It is a very famous town with Sweden's largest university and finest Gothic cathedral. It is the seat of the Archbishop of Sweden and the country's foremost centre of learning. Traditionally, life in town has revolved around the cathedral and the university.

Students are spread all over the world from Uppsdale University. I know Herr Erik Frykman, who is in charge of the Swedish department at King's College, Old

94

Aberdeen, is a fully qualified lecturer in the Swedish language and literature. He seems to be a brilliant scholar, and used to study English, German and French at the University in his student days.

Emanuel Swedenborg reigned from 1688 to 1772. He had faithfully lived and worked as a world-famous natural philosopher in Uppsala. He was born in Stockholm on January 29th, 1688, but spent his life mostly in Uppsala, where his father, Doctor Jesper Swedenborg, subsequently was a professor of theology at the University and also a Bishop of Skara. His father was under suspicion of heterdoxy, as he placed more emphasis on the cardinal virtues of faith, love and communion with God than on dogma.

Late in life, Emanuel Swedenborg wrote to Oetinger that "he was introduced by the Lord first to the natural sciences, and thus prepared, and indeed, from the year 1710 to 1745, when heaven was opened to him." Before his illumination he had been instructed by dreams, and enjoyed extraordinary visions, and heard mysterious conversations. According to his own account, the Lord filled him with His Spirit to teach the doctrines of the new church by the Word from Himself; He commissioned him to do this work, opened the sight of the Spirit, and so let him into the spiritual world, permitting him to see the heavens and the hills, and to converse with angels and spirits for years, but never received anything relating to the doctrines of the church from any angel but from the Lord alone while he was reading the Word.

There is a Swedish postage of Emanuel Swedenborg in my big stamp album at home. He has a heavy forehead with twinkling eyes.

Lavrentius Petri, Archbishop of All Sweden, edited, or

96

I myself do not wear wigs

Anno ætatis 80.

The Honble EMAN.^l SWEDENBORG

Born at Stockholm Jan. 29th 1689, died in London March 29.th 1772.

C.&A.Baos sculp.

superintended, the translation of the Bible published at Uppsala in 1540. He also wrote many psalms. He was a person of temperance. There are many historical and ecclesiastical interests in Uppsala.

I proceeded northwards to Gavle, where I reached the house of Herr Sven Ove Silfverberg and Frau Lilly Silfverberg. They are both Swedish deaf mutes.

*   *   *   *

JUNE 10. I had a good breakfast with Herr and Frau Silfverberg in their small kitchen.

We went down to visit a seaport and a station before returning home for our dinner. Their lounge is replenished with many souvenirs. A pocket flag is probably a Swede's favourite souvenir above all kinds of souvenirs. Frau Silfverberg kindly offered me a Gavle flag. I shall keep it as a souvenir.

Herr S.O. Silfverberg offered me the hospitality of a holiday bungalow about two miles off Gavle, but the time does not permit me to stay there for one night. It was built by the Gavle deaf and dumb associates themselves. It is a wonderful building.

I carried on through the great forest to Soderhamn. I was amazed to see the beautifully low falls above the bridge before reaching Soderhamn. I felt cold in the frosty air.

At Soderhamn I visited Herr S.O. Silfverberg's personal friend. I received a hospitable offer to stay in his beautiful home overnight.

The ancient church of Soderhamn was erected in 1685. It is still the local place of Christian worship. Soderhamn is a ship-building town.

*   *   *   *

JUNE 11 . I proceeded on my way to Sundsvall *via* Enanger, Husiksvali and Njurunda from Soderhamn. Passing Njurunda I saw a number of logs floating in the Ljungan River.

I arrived in Sundsvall, where a Clerk offered me a bed for one night at the Holmsgarden Hospital. I went out walking on the promenade to see boats for a short time. Afterwards I returned to the hospital.

After a good hot bath I went upstairs to bed, and read by the electric light over my bed.

Sundsvall was almost totally destroyed by fire in 1888, but has been rebuilt as one of the finest towns in Sweden.

*　*　*　*

JUNE 12. I am still having a rest in this hospital. Superintendent Leif Matthison officially visited me and I asked him to sit on a wooden form with me. The windy air warmed my skin beneath the hot sun during a talk with him. He is in charge of the Sundsvall Deaf and Dumb Institute.

A clerk brought a local reporter and his photographer to the office, where they had an interview with me about my Continental experience. They asked me: "Are you an English gentleman?" I promptly replied: "No. I am a Scotsman, which is different altogether." Outside I was snapped standing with my bicycle behind the cherry tree. They said that I may be mentioned in the Sundsvall newspaper tomorrow morning, as the Sundsvallian readers will be very interested in my story.

Herr Andrew Wedin was brought to me by a clerk, for he will help me to understand what he writes during my stay in this hospital as he is a fluent English speaker.

Better to wear out

shoes than sheets

Andrew showed me the lovely chapel. A number of patients and old-age pensioners go to this Gospel meeting every Sabbath Day. He told me of his holiday story in the Belgian Congo. It was good and interesting. He is a painter by trade.

A clerk asked me to go upstairs with him to see two patients whom I commenced a friendly talk with.

He said: "One of those patients has been suffering from his illness for thirteen years. He is thirty-three years of age."

At one o'clock I went downstairs with Andrew to the dining-room, where we had a good dinner together.

I left Sundsvall for Veda *via* Harnosand and Bergwforsen in the afternoon. In the northern surroundings of Veda I spent my sleep in the doorless and windowless condemned house among the trees. The windy wave of fresh air freshened my nostrils during my sleep all night.

*   *   *   *

JUNE 13. I happened to find a Swedish worker coming here before the commencement of his scarping work in the morning and I moved towards him from gathering my belongings. Afterwards I made friends with him and showed him my story cutting in Sweden.

I proceeded on my way to Gullanget *via* Vibyggera, Bjasta and Ornskoldsvik. The dull sky was looking merciless with its mercenary blackish clouds.

At Gullanget I pushed the light bell with my right thumb at the front door of the wooden council house, where Herr Sigurd Marklund and Frau Martha Marklund were residing. Frau Martha Marklund opened the door and

greeted me cheerfully, and then showed me into the lovely kitchen.

Subsequently Herr S. Marklund came home for dinner after twelve o'clock. He was very pleased to meet me. Afterwards he returned to his work. He is a cardinal leader amongst the local deaf and dumb associates.

After supper we cycled down to Ornskoldsvik, where we met the editor for the "Ornskoldsvik Allehanda." He invited me to be photographed when I sat down reading the local daily newspaper on an armchair: He showed me the best quality of photograph by a young Swedish technician. He gently laughed and said to me: "He has constructed a wireless and a gramophone desk himself." The Ornskoldsvikian readers may, in interest, read about his work and skill tomorrow morning.

We went outside and then began to cycle down to the wooden seaport, where we met a few deaf and dumb associates. Herr S. Marklund thrice swung the engine with a handle in his own motor boat, but it was somewhat troubled. Later on, it started to run well when the tank had been filled up with oil!

We made a good trip to the Ornskoldsvik Firth but it began to pour with rain. We fairly hurried home under darkish grey clouds. Gullanget stands about one mile off Ornskoldsvik. I do not think it is one of the Ornskoldsvik suburbs, but a proper self contained village.

Frau M. Marklund kindly offered us each a cup of coffee and biscuits in the kitchen. She charmingly said to me: "I have baked all different kinds of biscuits and cakes myself." She is very simple and homely and her smile is one of pure Christian love.

I saw numerous skis when I left my bicycle in the very

Lady Smiling

This is a swedish lady
miling at Jim.

clean cell. There are no cobwebs at the corners in this cell. I found no spider or beetle round about. Frau M. Marklund said to me: "Our skis are not to be used until the winter."

She showed me to the beautiful bedroom. I felt like a royal Prince when I enjoyed reading a book in a comfortable bed below the beautifully designed electric lamp standard. Everything is beautiful, new, and strictly clean and tidy in the whole room.

*   *   *   *

JUNE 14. I rose in the sunny morning. I went upstairs to the toilet, where I had a wash. I saw my photograph beside a young Swedish technician's on the front page of "Ornskoldsvik Allehanda."

After breakfast I went on the pleasant promenade down to Ornskoldsvik, where I had an interview with a bank manager. Afterwards I returned to Gullanget for my dinner.

The deaf and dumb Associates' Committee was held in the home of Herr Granlund and Frau Asta Granlund in the evening.

*   *   *   *

JUNE 15. Umea is a productive commercial town. This town (16,000 population) is rich in memories of the war of 1809, when it was occupied by the Russian warriors.

I reached Umea with its colourful homes, trees, vast pastures, etc., from Ornskoldsvik *via* Husum, Nordmalina and Hornefors in the direction of the east coast.

I am still in Umea. I have had a chat with a Swedish serviceman. He is home on leave from the Swedish National Armed Forces. He is neatly dressed in the khaki

... ... gärna bli fotograferad med ... ...
... nagra enstaka svenska ord. Dä...... ...
... ...ska och franska.

Dövstum skotte på
ykel genom Europa

uniform of a corporal. He is a man of considerable intellect.

At times during the supper hour a Finnish-born married lady of sorrows and joys told me a mournful story of her daughter. She was compelled to go with her children across the Gulf of Bothnia to Sweden because the Russians made a terrible nuisance in occupying part of Finland. Her daughter was fortunately adopted by a wealthy Stockholm couple in Stockholm. They were granted special permission for looking after her daughter for a short while. When the Russian-Finnish war was over she would hardly go back into her mother's arms owing to the exalted position of her foster parents, and flaunted her beautiful garments before her mother who had visited her in the Swedish capital.

I felt sorry for her daughter's disobedience against the Christian parental rules. I said to myself: "I hope she may change her mind, return to her mother and then kiss in love."

* * * *

JUNE 16. In the morning air I felt that I was well strengthened to carry on to Skelleftea *via* Robertsfors and Burea.

Arriving upon my bicycle very easily at Skelleftea, after a short visit to a deaf and dumb Swede and his white-haired wife in Burea, I was enthusiastically and joyfully welcomed by Herr Gustav Brannstrom and Frau Gerda Brannstrom.

Though we had great fun and joy in homely conversation with one another, we never thought of looking up at the clock until one o'clock in the morning, when we felt tired and sleepy. That was how at home they made me feel.

I went straight to my small bed beneath the roof of the big wooden house after a hot bath, where I fell sound asleep. Tomorrow will be spent in visiting friends in a picturesque dwelling place.

*   *   *   *

JUNE 17. This is the Sabbath Day, known as the Lord's Holy Day. Everything is very quiet, calm and peaceful. There are a lot of young and old Swedish people who attend the Lutherian Morning Service. They look like pretty and colourful flowers during their walk to the church. They are a very clean race. They remember the Scriptural rule "Remember the Sabbath Day, to keep it holy. Six days shalt thou labour, and do all thy work. But the seventh day is the Sabbath of the Lord thy God; in it thou shalt not do any work, thou, nor thy son, nor thy daughter, thy man-servant, nor thy maid-servant, nor thy cattle, nor the stranger that is within thy gates. For in six days the Lord made heaven and earth, the sea, and all that in them is, and rested the seventh day; wherefore the Lord blessed the sabbath day and hallowed it." I like to say that "God Sondag" is written in Swedish for Good Sunday.

Herr Gustaf Johansson and Herr Allan Marklund, his popular chum, shouted with a good laugh: "O Cheerio! Good morning to you all" when they came in to visit us. Herr and Frau Brannstrom introduced them to shake hands with me. The very striking bond of social and religious traditions in hope, in love and in freedom has been firmly established between them and the family of Brannstrom for many years. They are all deaf and dumb like myself.

Herr Gustaf Johannson had recently shown me his small

licence card, and informed me that a portion of his life's blood may be transfused for the Swedish Transfusion Aid. He is a tailor by occupation.

In the sunny afternoon we walked out round town, where the old-fashioned homes built by the Lapps were on public display in the open air. The local park with flowers and trees was lovely.

*　　*　　*　　*

JUNE 18. I had to eat plenty of hot pancakes and drink coffee at breakfast time with the Brannstrom family in the kitchen. Personally I found that Frau Gerda Brannstrom was a grand and capable cook. I recognised her as one of the finest and best conversationalists I had met in my life. I shall never forget the refreshing picture of her and her good husband all my days.

In Sweden, coffee ("kaffe") is almost a national drink and very much liked. Tea ("te") has not gained the same popularity as coffee. Now I am a great coffee drinker since I attempted the first taste about twenty-nine days ago.

At 8 a.m., we went up to the station, where we expected to meet their son and daughter. Afterwards we greeted them and took them home with us after their arrival from Stockholm by electric train. They are intelligent school children. They are beginners in English at school. I myself had never been taught how to write and read Swedish at school in Scotland. Herr Gustav Bannestrom mended my khaki knickers well. He has got a business on his own account as a tailor.

The local editor mentioned that I had been well looked after by the Brannstrom family for nearly three days. I e must b

told him that I was going to write a book about this Continental trip when I reached home again.

I said good-bye to them all when I began to run away to Munksund near Pitea, where I was invited to stay in the country home of Herr and Frau Berglund for one night. I thought they were very humble but no gainsayers or backbiters. Frau Berglund has had to come over to Swedish soil, where she was married to her Swedish husband, from Finland, a few years ago.

* * * *

JUNE 19. I carried on to Lulea *via* Pitea. At Lulea, large quantities of the Norbotten ores are shipped from this port. The arrangements for shipping the ore at the Svarto Quay are well worth seeing.

I should renounce my intention of pedalling to see the Finnish consul at Haparanda, the most northerly town in Sweden, for permission to enter the Finnish Lappland for North Cape, because of certain risks and difficulties — food shortage especially. Also it would be a little difficult, I think, to find a cycle repairer in the wilderness if my cycle happened to break down there. In fact, a long journey would make me feel deperately lonely when I found no Lapp tribe or house for many miles. To reach North Cape from Rovaniemi is about 250 or 300 miles. I am ashamed of myself for not having more faith.

At Lulea at twelve o'clock, I had a good dinner, namely: fried herrings, boiled potatoes, coffee and plain biscuits. "Sill stekt, potatis kokt, kaffe och kex" in the home of Herr Ruben Halibom and his wife. It reminded me of breathing the old Scotch smell of fried herrings. Herrings had been imported to Northern Sweden from the

I'm so sad I've lost my hope.

Norwegian fishermen. I am very fond of eating fish myself. I am descended from Scottish herring catchers in Cairnbulg, Aberdeenshire.

After dinner I paid a visit to friends in town. Now I changed my route which may take me up to Harads *via* Boden from Lulea. I took another road to visit Herr Goran Nilsson and his stout helpmate in a country village when I was in Boden. A friend is better than a few miles of journey which in time means little or nothing. I pedalled with full strength to Harads, where I tried to buy something to eat, but the shops were all closed down in the evening.

I sought somewhere for my bed and found a shed which was covered with strong logs, and was clean and healthy.

No-one disturbed me so I slept deeply and comfortably upon plenty of straw inside the shed, and needed no blankets. I had chosen the shed rather than my own tent because it would be very easy for me to get out of that place without a lot of preparation tomorrow morning. I am just lazy. There were many sheds in which grass, I believe, is to be stored for winter.

* * * *

JUNE 20. At about half-past six, in the bright, sunny morning, I awoke with a terrific thirst. "In the land of the Midnight Sun, the number of hours of bright sunshine in summer is greater than it is either in Rome or Madrid." I can prove this to be true. I lifted a bottle of water out of my rucksack for a drink as I felt a bit sick and dizzy.

I gathered all my belongings and started to cycle over the Arctic Circle to Jokkmokk *via* Vuollerim. Jokkmokk is very close in the neighbourhood of the Arctic Circle. I was

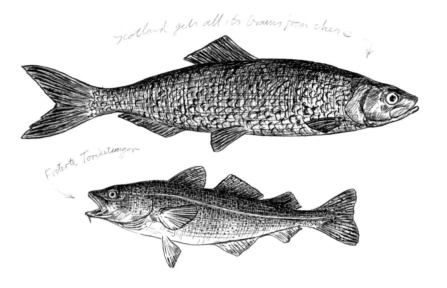

scotland gets all its brains from ches

Fyfertr Torskitungor

amazed to look at a young Lapp lady as she left the baker's shop for a walk home. She was dressed in a blackish-blue coat, black shoes and nylon stockings. A rich red ball in the top of her blackish-blue hat looked something like the Scotch thistle.

It has been a wonderful experience to see numerous Lapp residents in the streets. At the moment they are not very far advanced, but gently and without undue compelling of their natural growth, they are being ushered by the Swedes into the Atomic Age.

Herr Ove Anderson and Herr Lennarth Didoff from Uddevalla, were the first young people I met a few minutes after my arrival in Jokkmokk. They flattered themselves by trying to speak a few words in English to me, since they had noticed a pocket Union Jack on the front of my bicycle, when they were proceeding towards me where I sat down eating biscuits at the low platform. They wondered if I was an Englishman by birth. I answered them: "No, I am a Scotsman." I had an enjoyable time with them. They were both University students, at present spending a holiday in town. They are not Lapps but Swedes. It reminded me of the Christian motto: "Let no one seek his own good, but let each seek that of his fellow men."

One said to me that he might go back southwards to the University for his civil engineering studies when his holiday was over.

As far north as Northern Alaska or the middle of Greenland, I left the well-built Jokkmokk for Porjus. I felt like a lost sheep while seeing no living being through the wild forest, but I carried on steadily to Porjus. I had to go on my way to visit my friends where I had coffee with them in town. The Jokkmokk Porjus road is made of thick

"No, I am a Scotsman."

scattered pebbles and ashes. It is no good for cycling on. Another road to Gallivare in the northern boundary of Porjus would suit a cyclist better.

Proceeding northwards on my run to Porjus a reporter and his photographer shouted at me, stopping me from their motor car. Afterwards they noted that I was a Continental tourist, and asked me questions about my trip for the Swedish daily news papers. I answered them that it was my hope that I would be able to travel northwards by cycle to North Cape *via* Hammerfest from Narvik. The primitive road which had been built by the Germans was the open way to North Cape during the second world war. Finally, I told them that I had not been tired at all, but they laughed so that I yawned naturally before my departure to Porjus.

To the west of the forest region, through which the road passes, lie the field. At no place in Sweden is the scenery more wild and magnificent than here in northern Lapland's mountain region. Trails and waterways, as well as tourist stations, made it possible to penetrate far into the heart of this untouched wilderness of which the greater part has been made into a National Park.

Proceeding northwards to Gallivare by cycle, I broke my journey and looked at the Lapp sleepers' tent below the low- slope of the road, thoughtfully and with interest. The lure of Lapland lies in its unspoiled natural charm and beauty and in the wonder of the Midnight Sun.

Certainly I discovered that the Universe of God must greatly, very greatly, be the most astonishing marvel of creation. I noted that the smell of Lappish snow must be the equivalent to the smell of Scottish snow when I cut off a piece with my hands. Snow lies among the fields on

either side of the road. I visited Mt. Dundret, known as "Mountain of the Midnight Sun," before arriving in Gallivare.

* * * *

JUNE 21. I arrived in Gallivare at 12.30 a.m., when the Midnight Sun still shone above the horizon.

I saw a young Lapp man in the centre of the town. He hid his youthful face shyly against the front window of the sport-seller's shop. He was nicely dressed in Lappish national costume. His blackish blue garments were heavy, thick and warm. His legs were wrapped in blackish-blue bandages. The red stripe in two-inch wide column round his neck to the cape of his chest, the other red stripes in half inch wide columns round his upper arms, the black stripes in each two-inch wide columns on the upper shoulders, the red stripes in two-inch wide columns on the semi upper shoulders, both alike front and back, the yellow stripes in one-inch columns on the low shoulders, both alike front and back, the red stripes in three-inch wide columns round his low wrists, and the yellow stripes in one-inch columns round his upper wrists, and the red stripe in two-inch column round his hips. His lovely cap was a proper American working man's cap, but a non-cylindrical red ball in the summit of his cap looks something like an ostrich-feathered helmet (the German Kaiser's Imperial helmet).

Nowadays the Lapps wear heavy working boots. They do not need the reindeer fur slippers, they are out of date. Tents, rucksacks, knives, etc., are on public display in the shops.

This community has, like the neighbouring mining

ape of his chest, the other red st
e columns round his upper arms
ach two-inch wide columns on th
red stripes in two-inch wide col
per shoulders, both alike front a
ipes in ...e-inch columns on the
ike f...d back, the red s
id... ...nd his low w
r... ...nch columns rou
...e in two-inch c
...cap was a proper A
...a non-cylindrical red
...ooks something like
...rman Kaiser's Im

settlement, Malmberget, grown up right beside the iron-ore deposits in the vicinity.

I arrived at Malmberget throughout the southern slopes of the mountain from Gallivare. It is majestically situated above Gallivare. At Malmberget I asked two pretty Swedish girls whether they could direct me to the shoemaker's house. Afterwards I found his home through their helpful guidance, but had to wait about half an hour till he arrived home after his special trip to see his home-fellows' football match at Lulea. He greeted me happily when he met me.

I had plenty of jokes and a merry chat with him. No-one can live without jokes. Coffee was ready for us before bed-time. At 3 a.m. we went into separate beds. We pulled down the blinds of the two tall windows in the same room. At 6 a.m. I disturbed him, and told him to get out of his bed for his daily work. He said that he was still tired and sleepy.

When we had finished breakfast we were ready to go out to his boot retailer's shop where he started his work. At the shop I sat down repairing my poor shoes beside him. A few times I noticed that he gave a broad yawn. I noted in interest that Swedish shoe craft is a little different from British shoe-craft. The stitching, sewing and finishing machines are different.

Next door to the boot retailer is the hearing confectioner, who has a sympathetic love for his deaf and dumb fellows in his village. He understands their sign language well. He loves to talk to them when he meets them in his shop or outside. He is a good man.

My shoemaker's name is Herr Einar Olsson. He, like myself, does not hear and speak. He is the head of the

Ext. wilderness, swedish lappland - daY

Archive footage of reindeer in Lappland. Wild animals roaming,
and yet confined.

                    HERR EINAR OLSSON (O.S.)
                         (subtitled)
              Lapp girls have time on their hands. Swedish bachelors
              won't wait forever.

Int. cAFE, GALLIVARE - night

                    HERR EINAR OLSSON
              Lapp girls may go against their parents' wishes and
              run off with the Swedes. Leaving many a Lapp bachelor
              desperately downhearted and in tears.

                    DUTHIE
                         (deflated, ashamed)
              That's ... unfortunate.

                    HERR EINAR OLSSON
              It's a long winter.

Int. Bedroom, home of herr einar olsson - night

DUTHIE and HERR EINAR OLSSON lie in twin beds, staring at the
ceiling. The strange light of the Midnight Sun keeps them awake.
They have been playing shadow puppets on the ceiling. They've
come to a natural pause.

                    DUTHIE
                         (shadow signing)
Would you say, Einar, that you were a good friend? Like one
who would keep you p all nightmaking you stoned and then not
allowing you to have any reciommpenzzz whatsoever. Problenmis
with th e sidti60es is that its tuil hereI. And frankly,
tishnalalalal, that I have forgotteb wjat it is tat is,
rsallyy really, impornatyoouoiuy. Not allowed to talk abour
that are we nowe,. ITls a twerrible llterary work but it IS
after all a NEW FORM. Can it not be? Say yiu and me goig
going out and making NEW stuff, gosd amine,

Malmberget Deaf and Dumb Laplanders' Association: "Malmbergets Dovstumforening Lappland."

I visited the warm hearted deaf mute villagers and their wives, who have good and clean homes. None of them is unemployed at present. They talk by one hand in spelling. I think they have got permanent jobs. Their names are Herr Hjalmar Andersson and Frau Sonja Andersson, and Herr Costa Erikssor and Frau Ebel Erikssor. Herr G. Erikssor took me with him to his father's large shop. He carefully interpreted to me in order that I might understand how to use the modern machinery. He showed me drawers, doors, windows, etc., being made by his work fellows. One of his fellows is also deaf and dumb Herr Paul Johansson. Herr G. Erikssor described him self as a highly-skilled joiner. The colour picture of factories and grasshopper is hung up in the office. It means that every tradesman must be warned strictly against leaving a job from factory to factory.

In the evening Herr Einar Olsson and his friends walked with us to the local park, where a courageous swan swam to meet us in the pond, climbed up and then stood among our feet upon the path. She has always been well-treated by the public.

Another man came to greet Herr E. Olsson and was asked to join us. He invited us to go to the cafe for coffee. I asked if they could tell me a story of Lapp's lives. They made good value of different Lappish stories for me, and I was very surprised to learn a lot about the Lapps and their civilised discipline.

There are colour portraits of Lapps on the wall at the cafe. Herr Einar Olsson always received many cheerful salutes from the villagers. Everybody loves to see his

famous smiling face, with pretty, red, fat cheeks. He is fifty years old but has never been ill in his life. I do not think he can boast himself a "show off" man. No, he is a very fine fellow and very generous.

*　*　*　*

JUNE 22. My trip to Gallivare from Malmberget was short, but I visited the ancient Lappish church. The old Swedish lady lent me an old-fashioned key for the church and I went along a narrow path to open a heavy door at the church. I entered to see the congregation. There are about four oil portraits of faithful ministers which are hung on the wall above the pulpit. These oil portraits are half spoilt, and are not clear pictures. Lapp worshippers sit down on hard forms when they have the time to attend the Lutheran service. I think their religious feelings are all right. They formally adopted Christianity in the eighteenth century, although attempts at conversion were made at a much earlier date. A large number both in Norwegian and Swedish Lapland belong to a curious Christian sect known as the "Laestadianer".

A flock of reindeer are transported annually to Gallivare in winter. Many Lapps, both sexes, stay in town. In fact, some Swedish bachelors catch nice looking young Lapp ladies for matrimony. Lapp ladies went against their parents, ran away with Swedes, and then became chosen wives, leaving many a Lapp bachelor desperately downhearted and in tears.

The Lapps' wealth depends on the number of deer he owns, for the people do not count their riches in terms of money, but by the number of reindeer in their possession. The rich Lapp will often own a thousand or more, and his necessities, mainly coffee, salt and snuff or tobacco, are so few that he will often increase the number of his herd by the money he makes in trading reindeer meat and furs, or by the tools carved from the animals' bones. Every part of the reindeer is utilised in some form or other, even the sinews and hair, the former being sold to merchants who export them for thread in surgery, the latter being disposed of in large quantities for the stuffing of life-belts, for each hair of a reindeer is a hollow tube, filled with air and unsinkable.

The old Lapp stood gathering fish with his hands and took them home from the grocer's shop when a Swedish lady let him have them at a reasonable price. His brown face with dirty teeth smiled at me when he looked me straight in the eyes. Most Lapps eat either raw or half-cooked fish as well as meat with their fingers. They do not need knives and forks. They know nothing about Swedish etiquette.

I returned to Malmberget shortly. Here I spent most of the evening in the home of Herr Gosta Erikssor and his Finnish wife. Regretfully I told Gosta that I would not like to keep his photograph in a boxer's dress because I have no time for boxers. He offered me one of his best photographs in a gentle man's dress. I told Gosta that he looked very nice in a gentleman's dress. I shall keep it myself.

*   *   *   *

JUNE 23. Herr Einar Olsson, Herr Hjalmar Andersson and his son have prepared their small belongings—food and fishing rods with hooks and lines. They are amateur anglers.

We pedalled down to Gallivare. At Gallivare the tall

This bracing holiday, Life.

, Lyngen.

driver lifted and put our bicycles on the radiator of the bus. We entered the bus and sat down on comfortable seats. We travelled past the beautiful modern school for the Lapp children about three-quarters of a mile off Gallivare to Pulijarvi near Svappavaara. The Gallivare-Svappavaara road is narrow and poor in the wilderness.

I do not know much about the Lapp children's rudimentary education, but I doubt if they must learn the Swedish grammar and language, arithmetic and geography. Their lessons are so simple.

At Pulijarvi we took a rest for a while in a neatly furnished kitchen at our lumberjack friend's big bungalow in the summit of the hill beyond the loch. Our lumberjack friend, whose name is Herr William Andersson, has a good working wife and a family of two chidren.

Herr W. Andersson's brother-in-law, Herr Johan Alrik Larsson undressed and entered the timber hut, the saunas or Lappish steam bath, with Herr Hjalmar Andersson. Mixed bathing is not unknown. They were to beat themselves with bunches of birch twigs when they sat down having occasional bowls of hot water on the timber platform. As they walked out of the torrid hut, they gasped as they faced the fresh air. They dressed and their cleansed faces and hands shone comparatively white and yellow as they came back to see us at the timber bungalow.

I fell in love with the Swedish way of cleanliness and manner. Cleanliness is a good defence of strength and health, as it makes the human body strong against diseases, louse, sickish smells, etc. They are mostly humble, sympathetic and good characters. They are gently, silent and polite-mannered people.

These Scandinavian people, with natural advantages,

have built up not only high mental and moral levels in personal life, but a material standard of life which also is remarkably high.

Sweden is the Prince of modern Scandinavia, because of her long-lasting peace during the Second World War.

Herr E. Olsson, Herr H. Andersson and his son pedalled away to another farther loch, where they spent the time angling. Herr H. Andersson told me of a short story. Last time he happened to find the Lappish bear's footmarks on the Swedish soil in the wilderness. As the bear left, breathing angry clouds of timber fire, as he and his angler friends slept like stones round the fire among the fir trees. The bear passed within a yard of these calm sleepers. He could have taken advantage of them and killed them if there had been no fire around them. The bear is a dangerous beast.

Herr W. Andersson's wife sent their little son to see if he could get reindeer meat for me, but they had none to sell. It is a pity that I have never eaten reindeer meat in my life. What a disappointment! Herr W. Andersson's wife had received orders from the Lapp customers to make garments for them. She is a good tailoress.

Herr W. Andersson, his wife and Herr J. A. Larsson walked with me down the footpath to the near loch. Herr W. Andersson put the motor engine in the stern of his own built boat as he moved it noisily. We sailed in the loch on a pleasure trip.

*　*　*　*

JUNE 24. We had a great time with them in the home of Herr W. Andersson until one o'clock in the early sunny morning. I managed to read the Swedish newspaper without an electric light in the bedroom upstairs. Looking

134

Fredhöis

UKEBLAD Skib o hoi

SOMMEREN 1951

Kr. 1,50

Nr. 20 - 1951

out from the window I watched that Midnight Sun above the horizon. I thought it would be worthy to snap the beautiful picture of the Midnight Sun. Its fiery shine grew beautifully bright and silvery before I went to my bed.

One second after these twenty-four hours the Midnight Sun starts to move forward to the horizon until it finally sinks below the horizon on the twelfth day of July.

In Scandinavian northern parts unroken daylight in summer and darkness in winter last from two to three months each. All preparations for winter are made during September and October, and full winter has set in by November.

As Herr Einar Olsson was a proper Charlie Chaplin he made us laugh a lot. We loved him with all our hearts. A good laugh knows no bitterness or jealousy.

It is a great thing that Herr W. Andersson, Herr John Alrik Larsson, and Herr Ragnar Kemi from Svappavaara had built a big timber bungalow in 1939 just before the commencement of the Second World War. Its architectural plan must be completely correct in measurement. Herr W. A. Andersson is an intelligent architect. I wished them my best congratulations.

In the sunny afternoon Herr Ragnar Kemi came down to see his old friend Herr W. Andersson. Herr Ragnar Kemi contemplated making his way back to Svappavaara with me by cycle in the evening when the sun was still shining brightly over the Lappish land.

At Svappavaara we were just ready to go to our separate beds in the same room upstairs in his timber house shortly after coffee. I felt I was not able to talk with him, because I myself was tired for want of sleep.

*   *   *   *

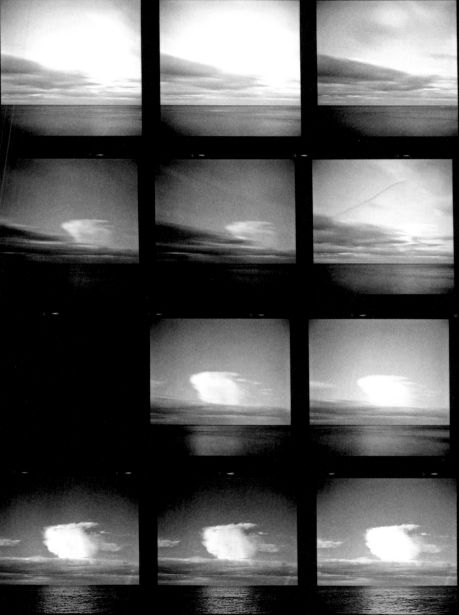

JUNE 25. I had a lift to Kiruna with a van-man who was transporting workmen to their jobs.

While passing the traffic slope I saw a small and old-fashioned tramcar. I went on my way to visit Herr Hjalmar Soderberg and Frau Maria Soderberg at their council flat, where I was invited to have a grand dinner with them, which was followed by most enjoyable conversation. They were both old-age pensioners, and both deaf and dumb. She said that potatoes would not grow in the Arctic. Perhaps she is quite correct. Tons of potatoes are exported to Swedish Laplanders and Lapps from many farms in sunny southern Sweden. I preferred the Scotch potatoes because the Swedish-grown potatoes are too thin and oval-shaped, but good to eat when boiled or fried.

She asked me to accept her kind invitation to stay here for a few days, to see more of Kiruna, and to make friends with Lapps at their tents, but I refused owing to the many invitations I had on route, and because my time was running short. If I accepted all invitations from friends of mine I would have come home very late from my three month trip.

I thanked Frau Maria Sonderberg for her loyal kindness and sympathy. I hoped my refusal might not injure her. She is a woman of good intentions and her humble husband too. Her neighbour came in to see her and during the course of conversation, she showed us the British post-card of the Flying Scotsman from her son who is spending his holiday in England.

At Kiruna reindeer fur-backed gloves, national flags, dolls in Lappish costumes, reindeer fur-sided handbags for the ladies, etc., may be seen in some shops. They are expensive, because the Lapps have made them by hand.

GLADESTE DUK

av et beskjedent motiv

Kiruna is the most northerly town in Sweden, and in the world the second town as regards the area, with 18,000 inhabitants. It began to grow in 1890 from a desolate waste, thanks to iron ore mining at Luossavaara and Kurunavaara, and grew very rapidly after the completion of the Narvik railway. A Christian Swede offered me a piece of Kiruna ore for a souvenir. Its length is two and three quarter inches. He described himself as a follower of Christ. The old Lapp woman sat down speaking a few friendly words to me at the railway station when I passed by. She is a souvenir seller. She mentioned these two big souvenirs—a reindeer fur-rug and a bust of reindeer being folded and tied on the handle-bars of my bicycle by a feeble and soft rope. She was perfectly attired in national costume.

At eleven minutes past three I began travelling by the stream-lined express train known as "SJ" to Riksgransen *via* Bergsfors, Tornstrask and Abiska from Kiruna. Waterfalls ran straight to the earth from the armour of the gigantic mountain's walls about three yards off from where I sat in the third class coach.

I saw the magnificent scenery of snow-clothed mountains throughout Lake Tornetrask. There are many low icebergs in Lake Tornetrask. I know nothing much about the ice and snow meltings there in summer because I am a stranger, in fact, the only people who know are the wandering Lapps.

At another station three Lapps entered the third class coach, where I sat down planning my future. I commenced chatting to these three Lapps, but they could not understand me. I felt sorry for them. They told me by means of signs of their remarkable experiences when reindeer hunting. I was surprised to learn a lot of strange ways from them. They can only speak their vernacular language, but they are far better off than the ancient Lapps who dwelt poorly and stupidly as a ship without rudder and compass.

One of these Lapps lent me his Lappish cap and I wore it like a British Field Marshal. It was only for fun.

Riksgransen is on the Swedish-Norwegian frontier. I arrived there in preparation for pedalling to Norway but I was compelled to continue by the same express train, because the narrow road to Norway was blocked with snow. From Riksgransen, the last Swedish rail way station and a well-known tourist resort with good facilities for ski-ing, the railway continues to Narvik in Norway.

The Norwegian passport officer asked for my British passport for examination. He congratulated me on my long journey to Narvik from southern France. The Swedish passport officer offered me a cigarette, but I refused it. I told him that I was a non-smoker. He asked me to come and see half-sunk German destroyers in the Narvik fjord through the window. I beheld narrow water-falls running down the walls of the mountains in the fjord.

I landed at Narvik in northern Norway for the first time, where I was ordered to bring my bicycle with all my belongings to the customs office for examintion. The first Norwegian person I met in town was a railway porter. He spoke English fluently.

I accepted the kind invitation to stay in the house of Herr Karl Lundgvist in accordance with his mother's wish. The Midnight Sun was hidden by the snow-capped mountains in the fjord.

* * * *

We'll pay for it

JUNE 26. Herr Karl Lundgvist's sweetheart works as a housekeeper to his mother. She is named Andrea Ellingsen. She was honest enough to tell me she did not bother to paint her face.

I asked her to be good enough to bring me the Norwegian Bible. As I picked a very striking scriptural verse out of the Old Testament and showed her it to read, she understood the meaning of the Divine morals clearly — "When thou art spoiled, what wilt thou do? Though thou clothest thyself with crimson, though thou deckest thee with ornaments of gold, thou rentest thy face with painting, in vain shalt thou make thyself fair; thy lovers will despise thee, they will seek thy life." Jeremiah IV, 30. Jeremiah was a great heroic prophet in the sight of the Lord. He (exalted by Jehovah) was the son of Hilkiah and a priest of the priestly city of Anathoth, three miles north of Jerusalem. He was called to prophesy when but a youth, in the thirteenth year of King Josiah (B.C. 628), and he continued to prophesy in Jerusalem and the other cities of Judah for forty years, until the final capture of the city (B.C. 588). No prophet reveals to us the inmost recesses of his mind more than Jeremiah. Remember that no prophecy in scripture is a matter of private interpretation; for never did any prophecy come by human will, but Jeremiah, sent by God, spoke as he was impelled by the Holy Spirit. Herr Karl Lundgvist and his nice-looking friends walked down with me to the small cemetery, where the British sailors and airmen had been buried among the Norwegians, and Germans too. There is a white-painted wooden cross on each British service man's grave.

Herr Karl Lundgvist pointed out his beloved father's

grave, and said that he had seen him shot down by Germans during the war.

The Germans took advantage of the Norwegian residents to dig and bury their own dead warriors in graves at the public cemetery.

I was happy to meet the Lapp with whom I had been in contact yesterday. At Narvik I was informed that there would not be any hope of getting into North Cape, "Nordkapp," from Kjelvik by road. I fear it may take two days or more in waiting to get a boat at Porsangvik for Kjelvik. In my opinion conditions will not be good enough to travel by foot to North Cape from Kjelvik.

I have never seen a Norwegian Lapp here, because at present most Norwegian Lapps are stationed in Finnmark. I think they may come back to the low Arctic Circle in winter as well as the Swedish Lapps. They have to guard their reindeers, and are hunters of wild beasts.

*   *   *   *

JUNE 27. I dined with Herr Karl Lundgvist's mother and her housekeeper in their home. I ate raw red fish with enjoyment.

I made a slight mistake by turning to another road, and had to return to the centre of the town from where I set out straight for Skarberget *via* Skjaersvik. I pedalled past the lazy rowing boats on the sand and was amazed to see the empty ruined submarine in dry dock above the fjord in an unexpected corner. I believe it was German.

I arrived at the Grindfjord ferry for Skiaersvik and sailed across a small firth to Skjaersvik only three minutes by boat. Half roof-shaped tall mountains of mighty granite

face the narrow dusty road, where I passed down to Skarberget. It was not good enough for cycling on. There are numerous and odd-shaped mountains. They are, I think, dangerous to climb. The granite is mostly greyish-black.

Another boat had just left for western Norway ten minutes before I reached the ferry at Skarberget. I had to sit down on a great stone, which I thought very lonely, and I had no human being to talk to in the sunny evening. Later I happened to find a new Swedish-made knife at the bottom of a great stone.

I pitched my tent beside the ferry upon the timber-fenced field for one night. Small, black insects, one quarter of an inch in length, flapped their wings about my naked legs through the open door of my tent when I lay reading a small magazine on the reindeer fur rug. Once, twice and thrice I cleared the insects away, but they returned each time.

I got out of my tent and went down the slope to the fastidious Norwegian shop. He sold me a chemical bottle. At my tent I poured a few drops of oil out of the bottle on my sorely pained legs, and rubbed them with my hands from knees to ankles. One bossy insect breathed an ugly smell of the oil and flapped away instead. A few minutes later his insect friends went away. Four days ago a nice Swede said to me that the insects may die of natural causes in twenty-four hours when they have filled their stomachs with human blood. They are drinkers of human blood. I myself know nothing about the nature of insects.

Reading and writing made good progress when I found no trouble with the insects. I slept peacefully all that night.

*　　*　　*　　*

JUNE 28. I packed up all my belongings after breakfast. I went back to the ferry where I sat down on the rocks thinking against the platformed road. Alas! I considered myself lonely when I had no-one to meet for about an hour. The stout Norwegian gentleman over six feet in height, came out of his big maroon-coloured modern car, in which his wife sat. He desired, in interest, to meet me and spoke a few friendly words to me. I greatly enjoyed a good conversation with him in English. I asked him a question: "Did any Norwegians go to Spitsbergen before?" "Yes," he answered, "but there are no churches, cinemas and towns, only the mines in Spitsbergen." He said that most Norwegian people are poor, very poor in Norway. He was a fluent English conversationalist. He had just arrived here after a long trip to Kirkenes which is situated on the Norwegian-Russian frontier in the south-east of Finnmark. He will drive with his wife home to Kristiansand through Norway.

The queue of luxury buses, cars, lorries and bicycle (mine), were held in a boat. I saw a working class man taking a woman into his small motor boat, and they began to sail around the houseless tall-walled mountain. I wondered if she was his certified wife.

Our ferry-boat ploughed through peaceful and silent waters beautifully, following the working-class man's sailing route, but he turned his rudder to the south after a mile. We were sailing northwards straight to Koranes.

We left Skarberget for Koranes at 10 a.m. I made friends with a skipper and his mates in the boat. Herr Norman Bakkejord from Narvik kindly offered me a lift in his own lorry. We were preparing to travel southwards by lorry to

Tippy

In Norway, I met a dog called
tippy he was a very nice dog which
I liked, I also miss home in
Inverallochy. The dog liked sausges
very much.

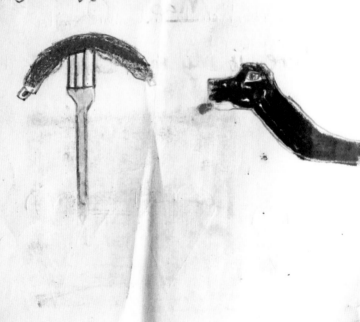

the Leirfjord for Rosvik. The lorry was in good running order.

In the boat from Leirfjord to Rosvik we hid our faces against the cold with scarves.

After our arrival at the Rosvik ferry we set out for Fauske. I saw a number of timber huts by the roadside, which are poor Norwegians' homes. Their roofs are covered with grass and dwarf trees. At Fauske we went shopping. The clean open air is refreshing all over the town. All streets are made of dusty earth. Again we intended setting out to Lonsdal where we stayed overnight.

Lonsdal is a mountain resort, 1670 feet above sea-level, and situated just beyond the Arctic Circle on the Saltfjell mountain plateau. Good trout fishing fine walking tours and a Lapp camp are a quarter of an hour away. It is the terminus of the Nordland railway. Here I had a grand supper with Herr Norman Bakkejord and his family in the modern hotel. The tall Norwegian bus driver came in to greet me, and take me to the beautifully furnished office where I was granted a Polar passport by two enthusiastic witnesses.

Lonsdal is neither a town nor a village, but an hotel and railway station.

*   *   *   *

JUNE 29. At sunrise I shaved off my black beard with my English-made razor. I went to the clean and fresh common spring and washed my face, arms and legs and drank cold water with cupped hands. Now I was neatly dressed.

Herr Norman Bakkejord and his professional boxer son came out of the modern hotel to meet me in the open air

Menu

LUNCHEON

"Smørrebrød"
Mixed cold meat
Waldorf salad
Pudding
Cheese and biscuits
Coffee

DINNER

Rolls and butter
Crème
Roast Pheasant
Pommes Rissolées
Jelly
Lemon pudding
Grapes
Cheese and bi
Coffee

Aquavit, Beer, Mil.

after their bed and breakfast, but the rest of his family had left them for Boda by train earlier. I looked up at a Norwegian flag waving at the top of the mast behind the hotel. In the sunny morning we departed for the Trondheim district.

Steadily we travelled southwards past the dial, which stands in the line of the Arctic Circle, about eighteen miles off Lonsdal; it is covered with a brown granite. We saw a number of walled timber fences about eight to ten feet in height while passing the rough mountainous road to Mo. No snow falls in summer but many high drifts remained from winter and I believe these fences act as shields against blizzards. They are about one hundred yards in length. At Mo we visited a beautiful fjord.

We departed to Trondheim, the capital of the Far North and the Gateway to the Land of the Midnight Sun, *via* Jemnes, Mosjoen, Levanger and Trondheim Fjord from Mo.

In the evening we arrived in Trondheim — we slept all that night. Trondheim's especial pride is the Nidaros Cathedral from the twelfth century, by any standards a magnificent architectural pile and one of the greatest medieval buildings of the North. Close to this impressive Gothic relic stands the 100 year old Arch-episcopal palace, and not far off the "Stiftsgaard", the largest wooden building in Scandinavia, built in 1770 and now used as a royal residence.

In Nideros Cathedral the present King Haakon and his wife, Queen Maud, had been crowned in 1906. Trondheim is situated on the same parallel of latitude as Iceland, Greenland, Northern Canada and Siberia, but bathed by the kindly waters of the Gulf Stream and vitalised by its warmth.

Olaf Trygvason, the Second King of Norway, founded the new city of Trondheim in the ninth century. He was a picturesque figure and described himself as a Christian in the Protestant faith.

Taking a long time before our arrival in Trondheim from the North, we went down to see the rushing water falls at Harran. Logs were floated wildly down noisy and smashing waterfalls spreading noise worse than a pipe band.

*   *   *   *

JUNE 30. In the early morning Herr Norman Bakkejord prepared to drive us home to Siggerud throughout Dovre Fell, Guderandsdale, Lillehammer, Hamar on Lake Mjorsa, and Oslo.

The Guderandsdale is known as "Norway's Valley of Valleys." It is long, broad, picturesque and beautiful. It presents the "front cover" scenery with smiling lakes, forests, quaint Norse farms, rivers and rushing waterfalls, and the whole valley is flanked by impressive mountain ranges. In countless ways the Guderandsdale is a true paradise for holiday-makers.

In the deep dusk we reached Siggerud, where I was invited to stay in the home of Herr Kristen Bekkejord for one night. His log-house is unhewn and well painted. His log-walled rooms are decorated with busts of animals. He has a wife and baby. He showed me his medals for his boxing championship in Norway.

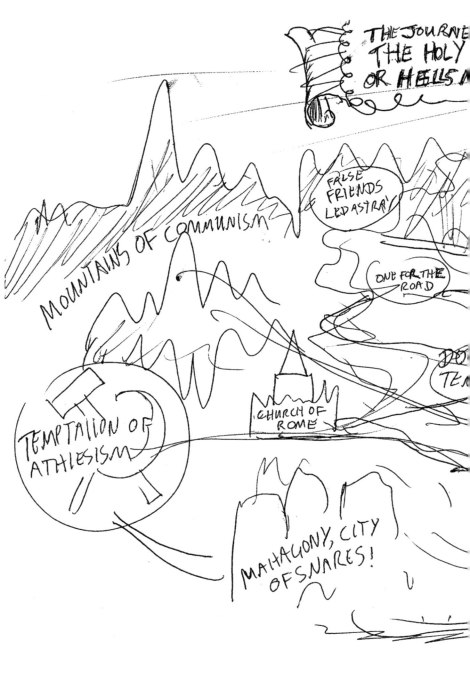

THE JOURNE...
THE HOLY...
OR HELLS...

MOUNTAINS OF COMMUNISM

FALSE FRIENDS LED ASTRAY

ONE FOR THE ROAD

DO...
TE...

CHURCH OF ROME

TEMPTATION OF ATHIESISM

MAHAGONY, CITY OF SNARES!

PUBLISHED BY THE METHODIST 'SCARE THE BEJEEZUS OUT OF THEM' SOCIETY OF

July, 1951

JULY 1. I pedalled northwards to Oslo in the morning where I paid a visit to the new Town Hall which has taken twenty years to build and has cost the Norwegians £1,500,000. A solid, twin-towered, brick-faced building faces the harbour, it is richly decorated inside and out. Not only has the new Town Hall fifteen stories, but the Norwegians claim that its clock — to be installed shortly — will be the largest in the European continent. The minute hand alone will be fifteen feet long, and the entire clock will be visible far out to sea.

The Town Hall will also boast an astronomical clock, fifteen feet in diameter, which will tell the time by the stars. A big dragon-hand will react to eclipses of the sun and moon. A globe representing the moon will revolve around the earth, the clock's centre corresponding to the movements of the sun, and show the phases of the moon. The astronomical clock will also show the date and altogether be provided with a multitude of astronomical subtleties which cannot satisfactorily be explained in a short article. The clock will be very ornamental and will glitter with gold and other colours. The figures have been modelled by Herr Nils Flakstad, who is a sculptor.

I saw the oil picture of King Haakon in the uniform of a Norwegian admiral at the Town Hall. The dweller by the fjord looked to the sea and across it for his inspiration, with the result that the Norse sea rover became the embodiment of maritime enterprise.

I visited the Deaf and Dumb Club in the northern branch of Oslo, where I stayed for two days. Herr Alf Melgaard narrated to me his experience in connection with

Norwegian and Swedish ski-ing colleagues at Jamtland in 1950. He showed me a modern cinematograph and a few film reels.

Herr Alf Melgaard's pretty fair-haired sweetheart from Bergen in Western Norway merely pointed out that she had found numerous snobbish Christiania citizens in Oslo streets. She prefers her home Bergen citizens best because they are mostly jolly, sportsman like and welcome lovers. It was her own saying. She has beautiful royal blue eyes. I believe she must be a direct descendant of those beautiful and gigantic Vikings.

During our walk to the city she pointed out places of interest and helped to interpret what I wanted to know. I rejoiced in a good time with Herr A. Melgaard and his sweetheart at their friends' flat in the evening. I tasted small fancy biscuits while drinking strong coffee with them. They were going to explain to me how to say the name of and understand each nation, Denmark, Finland, Norway and Sweden, by their signs. Example: To open your right thumb and second-third right fingers and to wave them past your waist from left to right means "Denmark." You may see that Denmark has the Jutland mainland, two large Funen and Zealand islands, and two North and Baltic seas. To show your white teeth and to dive your left or right dancing fingers from your teeth into your chest means "Finland." You may see snowfalls on the Finnish soil in cold winter.

To shut your right second-third fingers, and to lift up and down two or more times means "Norway." You may see that waterfalls can be seen on the summit of the tall mountains in the Norwegian fjords. To put your right fingers' ends on your left wrist, and to lift by closing your

right fingers' ends in the air means "Sweden." You may see that a long time ago the male Swedes used to wear reindeer fur overcoats in the cold climate.

The Danish, Finnish, Norwegian and Swedish sign languages, I have found from route to route, are so elementary and easy to learn, but there are no advances in the complete standardisation of Scandinavian sign languages.

My Norwegian friends in Christiania are all deaf and dumb, but smartly intelligent and knowledgeable. Oslo, the capital of all Norway is known as Christiania.

At the Royal Palace the Norwegian soldiers wear black bowlers within each feather-stand. I wondered whether it must be the black-dyed or natural black ostrich feather. They march past the King's residence.

*   *   *   *

JULY 3. I went back past the Akershus Castle to the quiet country road where I turned along another road for the south. I found the French screw which was troublesome and rotten at the back wheel of my bicycle and adjusted it. Afterwards I cycled away. I enjoyed pedalling down the south throughout the beautiful plain to Sarpsborg *via* Moss. I landed at Sarpsborg to which Magnhild Martinsen's charming brother kindly offered me a hearty invitation to stay overnight. Magnhild Martinsen kindly brought me to visit her poor white-haired father who has been ill and is still lying in bed. It was very thoughtful of her to ask me to talk to him for a short while. She has good parents and is very lucky.

Magnhitd Martinsen commented that no friend of the two Norwegian and Swedish peoples could find a friendly word to say in favour of their social and political continu-

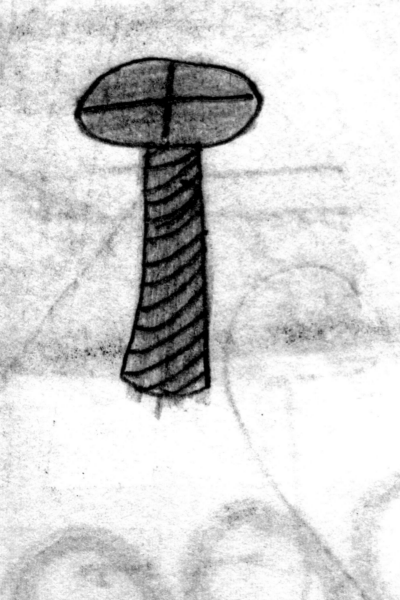

Turn, turn, turn . . .

ance. Many Norwegian people avoid meeting the Swedish people at the border, because they think the Swedish people are deeply hard to please, and are very proud.

Fortunately I enjoyed a good fish soup with Magnhild Martinsen and her parents in the kitchen. The Norwegian people's cheeks are naturally purple.

The Norwegians obtain reindeer meat in winter, but not in summer.

*   *   *   *

JULY 4. I reached the Norwegian-Swedish frontier at Svinesund, where I was asked again for my British passport by a Swedish passport officer through a Norwegian passport officer's strict permission over this modern beautifully built bridge above the wide river.

I cycled down to Uddevalla *via* Tanum, Hallevadsholm, Dingle, and Mimkedal. At Tanum there is the parish of Tanum which is usually rich in relics from the Stone Age, Bronze Age and Iron Age. The Bronze Age rock carvings are very remarkable. About 300 are known.

The ordinary literary language as it is officially styled, or the Norwego-Danish as it is scientifically termed, or "Riksmaal," in colloquial speech, is the Norwegian variety of the Danish language which came in during the union with Denmark "Danmark" (1380–1814). The Norwego-Danish language is still nationally spoken in modern times. Many Norwegians can speak English fairly fluently. I have no idea how quickly they could manage to master the English grammar and language, but I imagine that most of them must be good learners of intelligence with a considerable speed of mind. As far as I know they are as smart as Swedes. Old Swedish, during its earliest

A good laugh knows no bitterness or jealousy

pre-literary period (800–1225), retains quite as original a character as Old Icelandic and Old Norwegian. Modern Swedish language has changed a lot since the thirteenth century. Some words of ancient derivation are still used in the language of to-day. I think Swedish literature must be remarkably beautiful to read.

At dusk I arrived at Uddevalla, where I pitched my tent for one night. Uddevalla is an industrial and shipping town. It is beautified by modern council houses, shops, etc. The population is 23,700.

*   *   *   *

JULY 5. At Uddevaila a Swedish cycle dealer removed a worn-out tyre from my bicycle and put a new tyre on the wheel. The old tyre I had brought in France two months ago, was of poor quality.

I set out to Gothenburg, "Goteborg" in Swedish, Danish, and in Norwegian, "Gothemborg" in French, *via* Ljungkile and Kungalv with the old fortress of Bohus. I got a little rest at Kungalv before going across the wide river with its island to Gothenburg.

About ten minutes after my arrival in Gothenburg, I accepted an invitation to sojourn in the beautiful home of Herr Kurt Ericson, his fair-haired, stout wife and their pretty bairns for two days. He asked me to come downstairs with him to the clean windowless cell, where he showed me some goodly upholstered armchairs. Upholstery is his evening hobby. I slept alone in a lovely comfortable bed in a lounge all that night.

A deaf and dumb Swede uses the most famous Churchill "V" sign in his silent language. A deaf and dumb British does not use it.

Gothenburg with 344,000 population is the second largest city in Sweden, and its most important seaport.

*   *   *   *

JULY 6. To the north is Bohuslan with its myriad barren islands whose cliffs are polished clean by the pounding of the waves. The fishermen's cottages huddle together in the protective lee from the fury of the wintry northern storms. But in summer Bohuslan is a playground for those who love its briny water and the hot sun beating down on granite slates worn to a silken smoothness by the waves. Here are the finest sailing waters in Sweden in the open sea or leeward of the sheltering island fringe. In Bohuslan, holiday life is bracing and health-giving at its many picturesque seaside towns and numerous thriving fishing villages along the skerried coast to the north of Gothenburg.

Frau Rosa Ericson and her bairn travelled with me by steamer to Bjorko, which is the largest of the Bohuslan's islands, *via* Hono H. Grato, Ockero, St. Varholmen and Kalvsuhd fishing villages. We landed at Bjorko at the timber pier round the fishermen's cottages. We walked up and down the footpath among the granite slabs to the large summer bungalow only five minutes from the pier. We greeted deaf and dumb visitors and members of the Association inside the bungalow.

The Gothenburg Deaf and Dumb Association own this summer bungalow named "Solhem." The Gothenburgian deaf mutes had constructed the bungalow in their spare time, putting in windows, doors, chairs, tables, main hall, recreation room, etc. The money was raised through a fund and many donations were given.

168

In the early evening, Frau Rosa Ericson accompanied me back to the pier, where I caught the steamer for Gothenburg. I waved my right hand at her as she stood on the pier waving and smiling at me. I had promised to meet her husband at the deaf and dumb club when I got off at Gothenburg.

I congratulate myself on having interested myself in him. He is a helpful friend to have. Herr Cark Hjort is an acting consul for the deaf and dumb who suffer in financial trouble through unemployment.

Herr Kurt Ericson dutifully took me away with him to catch a tram-car home when they finished business at the meeting.

*　　*　　*　　*

JULY 7. Gothenburg was established by Gustavus Adolphlils in 1619; it was from the first designed to be fortified, a town of the contemporary name, established on Hisingen in 1603, having been destroyed by the Danes during the Calmar war. I am told that the Danes used to light fires when invading the neighbourhood of Gothenburg.

I am going to translate the copy of a marvellous sort of Carl Gustav Gromeberg into English from a book named "Dovas Arsbok, 1951–52."

Translation: "In wonderful summer, 1950, Carl Gustav Gromeberg's name was widely mentioned in newspapers. He is completely deaf. He has successfully gained the lower certificate for perfect pronouncement in English and in German.

There was no second scholar like him after his examination in Sweden's deaf population. He was assisted finan-

169

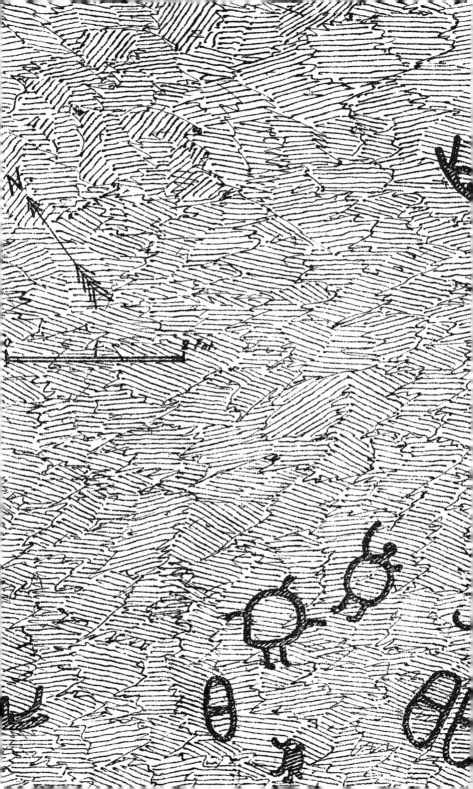

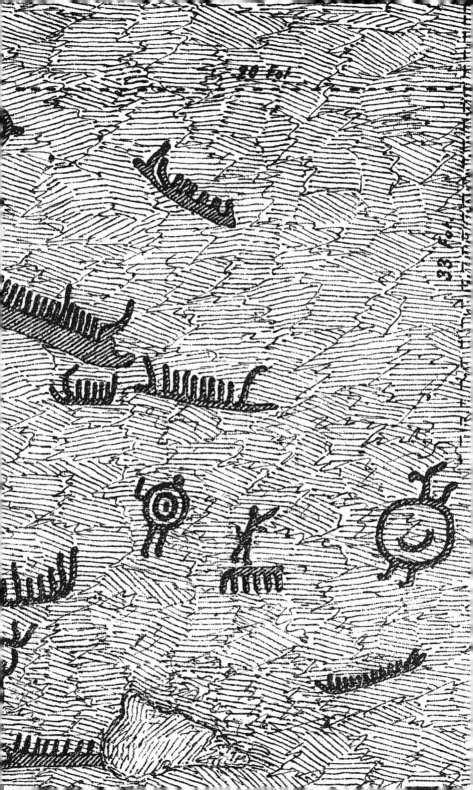

cially to travel to the United States of America by the Swedish Deaf and Dumb Association's and the Carlborgsson's Fund and Donations.

Gromeburg was born in Chagmrya outside Falun in Dalarna, one of the Swedish counties, in 1930. He lost his mother when he was a little child. He was looked after by his uncle and aunt. He lost his hearing when he was 11 years of age.

This unique university college for the deaf and dumb is situated in Washington and is the only one the world has possessed. There are seventy-five students in the same preparatory class, but no other student received the honour in promotion above all the others in the class."

Dr. W.R. Roe, Ph.D., author of "Peeps into the Deaf World," "Anecdotes and Incidents of the Deaf and Dumb," "Snapshots of the Deaf," "Our Deaf and Dumb," etc., once said that missionaries, architects, sculptors, contractors, electricians, fruit farmers and at least one lawyer are to be found amongst the college's former students.

I remember the story of a deaf mute bank manager who was in control of a large staff of normal people.

I hope Carl Gustav Gromeberg may graduate one day. Carl Gustav Groneberg whose remarkable article "Gatuliv pa 'H'-gatan" with seven illustrations is published in the Dovstummas Tidskrift—1891–1951 (20 issues per year). It tells about the American social and commercial life during his sojourning at Gallaudet College in Washington.

In preparation I gathered all my belongings before making a long journey to Halmstad, *via* Molndal, Lindome, Kungsbacka, Frillesas, Varberg, Marup, Falkenberg and Gullerandstorp in the morning.

I reached Halmstad on my way to visit a deaf Swede

"All of the children of silence must
must be taught to sing their own song."

whom I had met in Gothenburg last night. His father and mother are regular members of the Salvation Army. I visited the Halmstad Deaf and Dumb Association's summer bungalow where I slept over night in my own tent beside another deaf mute Swede's tent below. That ground was not so bad to pitch on. I gently turned and talked with several inmates till dusk.

A German-born wife from Stockholm pointed out that two Swedes will very soon come over to stay with us when they land at Halmstad by boat from Stockholm. There are a few Stockholm guests with her in this bungalow for their holidays. This bungalow is situated in Ekelanga, about one and a half miles off Halmstad and about five minutes from the sea. It is called "Tallvik." It contains five rooms and there is a log hut, which includes one dining room and kitchen.

Halmstad is a seaport, county capital and garrison town, with a population of 34,000.

*   *   *   *

JULY 8. I went back to Halmstad before setting out to Halsingborg *via* Laholm, O Karup and Angelholm in the noon. I tasted ice cream at Angelholm. I was charmed by the local inhabitants in town.

I arrived in Halsingborg to visit the modern home of Herr Otto and Frau Saly Ternay, where I had coffee with them and their friends—Herr Erik Herimer and Frau Magnhild Herimer. Frau Sally Ternay told me that she was expecting her husband home from his holiday in Skane. Again she smiled and said to me that she loves making him very welcome. He is an assistant missioner in

Halsingberg Deaf and Dumb Association, which was founded in 1925. This is the twenty-sixth youngest association in Sweden.

We walked down the side street to the harbour, shook hands, and then he wished me a hearty farewell when I commenced sailing across the quiet sea to Helsingor. The Swedish mariner inspected and stamped the pink-shaped mark of departure date in the twelfth visa of my British passport.

Standing on the deck behind the cabin in the steamer I looked down into the mirror of the sea, that danced with the bright lights from the electric lamp standards at Halsingberg. Midnight approached and the low sky became shaded by black clouds.

*   *   *   *

JULY 9. At Helsingor the Danish mariner asked for my British passport for examination. Another sullen Danish mariner sharply complained against me for taking a reindeer fur rug away. But I explained to him that it was used for my tent mattress. Well! he permitted me to go with it out of the exit. Here now is Denmark. At Helsingor I was tired and sleepy. I went somewhere to spend a few hours in sleeping. In the daylight I went back on a run to Copenhagen, "Kobenhavn," such as I did twenty-four days ago. At Copenhagen I looked knowingly around the beautiful spires after my arrival. The word "Copenhagen" means "the merchants' harbour" and the geographical position of Copenhagen is a dominating one for trade in the north of Europe. It is known as the "Paris of the North".

The ancient Vikings must be said to be the original

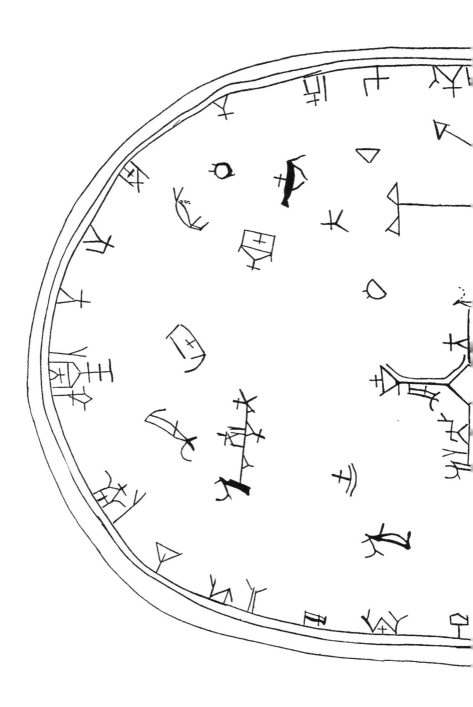

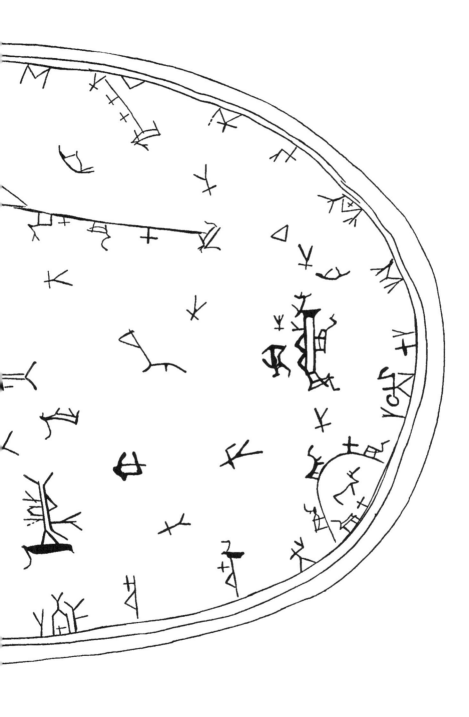

founders of Copenhagen. Signs of habitation can be traced back to the days of the Vikings. However, it was not until 1167, when Bishop Absalon constructed his citadel on "Holmen near the Sound" that Copenhagen became a town. Copenhagen is the capital and government seat of Denmark.

I contemplated sojourning at the old-fashioned flat of Herr Neils Jorgen Kronhoff and his twice married wife. His wife had been a widow before her marriage to him and is a native of the island of Langeland, where she had spent her childhood days. Her parents and her own little sons live on the island of Funen, which in Danish means "Fyn."

Herr N. J. Kronhoff is a habitual laugher and loves making jokes with his friends. I was surprised to learn that he was unfortunately tempted to start smoking a pipe. I have nothing against him for as far as I know the Bible says nothing about smoking. Truthfully I still think it must be a sinful curse. I however remembered that he was an enthusiastic non-smoker during my previous holiday at Veile in the mainland of Jutland.

We went on our way to visit our friends' home from the Institute.

*   *   *   *

JULY 10. I was preparing to make my way to visit the Grundtvig's Memorial Church, which is picturesquely placed in an imposing organ-like silhouette.

Afterwards I enjoyed looking around inside the beautiful modern ecclesiastical buildings when the Lutheran service was over. What a marvellously mighty architecture!

I cycled away to visit Herr Niels Jorgen Kronhoff's cheerful-hearted aunt who is a sister to his mother. I

I think it is a lot of nonsense and rubbish

admitted having interest in the Society for the Aid of Distressed Mothers and Children, founded in 1904, and also in the Society for the Aid of Distressed Single Women with Children, founded in 1905.

Danish women, whether married or unmarried, get every assistance in dealing with the many problems connected with childbirth from a voluntary institution which enjoys statutory backing and wide public sympathy, helping every mother or expectant mother with all her problems and difficulties.

Frau Vera Skalts, Director of the Mothers' Welfare, says in her book, "The Unborn Child," in advertising and assisting others, it is the human touch that counts. Nothing could be truer. Without deep human sympathy, without a constant desire to help and avoid dead routine, the work of the Mothers' Welfare would quickly lose its value. The institution is a much blessed society. During the pouring night rain I put on my cape as I walked out to meet my other old friend. But his wife told me that he was absent. So I returned home where I stayed happily with Herr N. J. Kronhoff and his wife all that night.

*   *   *   *

JULY 11. Leaving Copenhagen, I set out for Korsor *via* Glostrup, Hedehusene, Roskilde, Ringsted, Soro and Slagelse. I arrived in Korsor, which itself is an important ferry station on the Great Belt. It has a new church with many old relics, a naval battery, and defensive tower from the Middle Ages.

I crossed the Great Belt by boat to Nysorg and beheld the town of Nysorg afar off. I now reached Nysorg.

Telling Dummy Jim's story

May 1951, a profoundly deaf Scotsman called James Duthie (known as Dummy Jim) cycled solo to the rctic Circle. On returning to Scotland, Duthie self-published a book about his travels called 'I Cycled into e Arctic Circle,' selling it door-to-door.

early half a century later, filmmaker Matt Hulse was given a copy of the book, and, inspired by Dummy Jim's ory, set about making a film with Deaf filmmaker and actor Samuel Dore.

3 years later, the film has finally reached the screen, receiving its world premiere at the Rotterdam ternational Film Festival in January and its UK premiere at the Edinburgh International Film Festival in June, here it was nominated for Best British Feature Film. BDN spoke to both Matt and Samuel about their urney, and the final film.

The royal castle at Nysorg built in 1170, is the oldest in Scandinavia.

I went homeward to Odense *via* Ullerslev and Langeskov by tracing the same main road back. During my run beyond Odense, angry lightning sometimes terrified me and I had to shelter from rain in a garage. Looking out of the entrance I lifted my eyes and looked upon the raging, boiling tosses of waters in the flat-tarred road.

I stayed about two hours in the well-covered garage before setting out for Odense when the weather was clear. But the rain still carried on. At Odense I was warmly comforted, and invited to stay overnight in the typical Danish home of Herr Hans and Frau Caroline Pidersen. He seems to remain as an old-age pensioner, but he still carries on working as a cigar manufacturer at the factory in town. He is looking after the deaf and dumb Danes' national health insurance cards from every corner of this island that is situated in the middle of the kingdom. Odense is Funen's capital and Denmark's third largest town (110,000 inhabitants). It is the birthplace of Hans Andersen, the world famous fairy tale writer. Hans Andersen wrote many fairy tales which are read to this day by adults and children all over the world. The atmosphere inspired Andersen to write his immortal stories.

*   *   *   *

JULY 12. At Odense Herr Hans Pidersen kindly recommended a guide to show me the deaf and dumb club. Afterwards she showed me round the lovely building.

I never noticed Hans Andersen's red tile roofed house when I was cycling back to the west past that place. I did not know that it was his own home. It was hard work

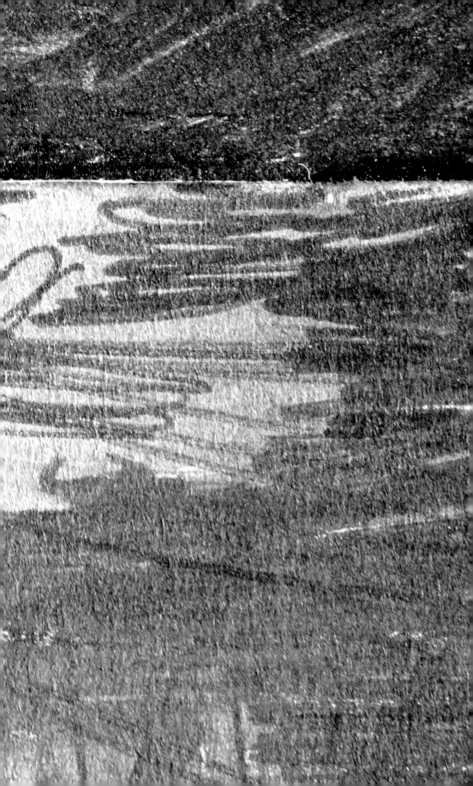

cycling to Middelfart on the Little Belt near the three-quarter mile long bridge, where I passed on to Frederica. This is Jutland now. At Frederica I went upstairs to visit the retired man at the Institution for the Deaf and Dumb. He has been granted an honorary medal for his long and faithful service amongst the deaf and dumb by the late King Christian the Tenth. He showed me a real medal.

I listened to his thrilling experience about hard hiking in Switzerland. I told him that I had been in Switzerland last year. I still think it is the most beautiful country in the world.

Herr Aage Thomsen introduced his Faroese-born apprentice to me at his tailoring workshop where he employed him. This tall and fair-haired Faroese whose name is Daniel Jakob Jensen, is a jolly young man and full of life. Herr A. Thomsen is a tailor master, and also a supreme head of the Danish Deaf and Dumb Association in Denmark. I accepted his invitation to return to my bed tonight. Herr D. J. Jensen, whose own people live in the Faroe Islands, can trace his ancestry back to the Vikings who came from Norway about the year 1000. Memories of the Faroese past are preserved in their language and customs.

I could not trace my ancestry back to the Norse Vikings or Picts or anything else, because of the failure to record births and marriages before 1855, and because of the frequency with which the name occurs in Rathen parish, even in the locality of Inverallochy in the north-east of Scotland.

I am James Duthie, descended from poor and hardworking Scottish fishermen. The sacred surname of Duthie is one of the oldest surnames in the two sided fishing village

of Cairnbulg and Inverallochy, known as " Invercairn." In the First World War my great and heroic father captured Herr Franz von Papen, former German Chancellor and Ambassador. After the war he was still a great man, a founder of the Westhaven harbour through Government grants. He was a great advocate. He was nicknamed "Peggy's James," well known in fishing circles.

The surname of Duthie is a shortened English form of the Gaelic MacGille Dubthaigh, "son of the servant of Saint Dubhthach." It occurs in Scottish records as early as 1492, then in Orkney. The surname of Stephen (my mother's maiden name), variously spelt, was introduced into Britain by the Normans, with whom it was a favourite.

In the evening Herr D. J. Jensen and I went to the town centre restaurant, where we met a company of deaf mute youngsters, and enjoyed coffee with them.

*   *   *   *

JULY 13. It is my common idea to point out that Jutland is properly the jester's head-moulded mainland. There are many brown coloured cows and horses in Jutland. The Danes treat their horses well.

On the evening of departure from Fredericia, it was light work cycling to the half-way of the south, but it became hard work cycling up the hilly road before Kolding, which is a fine seaport. I dined with Herr M. Madsen there. I used to be well acquainted with him. He is a wealthy shoemaker in his own work-shop at Fredericia. He is a fine friend to have.

At Kolding I willingly decided to spend the night at the house of Herr Carl F. Christensen, his model wife and their family. I found them hospitable and good.

Home

* * * *

JULY 14. I purchased expensive khaki knickers at the Danish draper's shop in the sunny morning. Afterwards I threw my old knickers into a fire and wore the new ones.

I paid a short visit to the hosiery, where I met Herr C. F. Christensen and his deaf mute mates. Everything was already stored in my rucksack at the back of my overloaded bicycle before I started to cycle southwards along the narrow and dusty road, where I turned left to go on to visit the Strendetgaard mansion. From the corner of the narrow road on the main Kolding-Haderslev road to the picturesque town of Haderslev on the first, it is almost about three miles.

At Strendetgaard a faithful governor was very pleased to meet me. He enabled me to see and talk to a few distressed deaf and dumb men. I was forced to take a goodly rest here until Monday. The cheerful old man took me with him to the stables, where he showed me a number of cows, pigs, geese, hens and cocks. The deaf mute workers are encouraged to continue easy jobs for their living. They are cared for in comfort and provided with clothes and food. In the evenings they read or do something else in a recreation room. They can ramble in the quiet grounds.

In the evening I enjoyed having a big dinner with this governor and his wife and their family in the drawing room at the mansion. I slept alone in a private hut all that night about 50 yards off the back of the mansion.

* * * *

'and he looked down toward Sodom and Gomorrah, and behold, the smoke of the land ascended like the smoke of a furnace.'

Genesis 19:28

JULY 15. I saw a pair of swallows feeding their crying babies in the nest on the electric lamp shade in a wash room. They flew away and returned through the open door. I attempted to pet a young pig, but he yelped at me for need of milk.

Strawberries, peas, cherries, gooseberries, black currants, apples, rhubarb, raspberries, etc., are easily to be found amongst the trees in the large garden opposite the back of the mansion.

Herr Henrik Boesen and his wife from Kolding came over to visit his father, who is the governor. They are both deaf and dumb. He presented me with a postcard-size photo of the mansion and great farm, which had been snapped from an aeroplane. Another maid presented me with two beautiful photos of the mansion.

Herr H. Boesen's hearing bachelor brother is a foreman, who rules the deaf mute workers. A foreman has no time for thinking of a future wife. He presented me with two photos, the first was of Royal Regiment in Scottish tartan kilts when they visited Haderslev. Since Viking days the relations between Scotland and Denmark have been peaceful. True, Danish-Norwegian sovereignty over the Orkney and Shetland Islands was for a long time a thorn in the flesh of the Scots, but an alliance entered into on the Danish soil in 1468 proved to be a bargain for Scotland.

An owl looked down upon me straight in the eyes. He flapped his wings and escaped to hide beneath the roof of the hay stable. The cheerful old deaf mute comments that an owl loves killing rats for his dinner, and has chosen the hay stable as a home of his own. He is a well-known bird in Strendetgaard.

* * * *

JULY 16. I returned in the morning to the main road for Haderslev, where a Danish cycle repairer fixed up one of the pedals on my bicycle. I set out straight to Aabenraa *via* Ov-Jerstal and Hoptrua. At Aabenraa, a beautiful seaport, I had a chat with a German-born wife who is married to a Danish deaf mute.

The weather was very warm and sunny during my run to Krusaa which is situated on the Danish-German border. At 11.30 a.m. a Danish passport official cleared my British passport after examination. At the border entrance a German passport official met me dutifully. I showed him my passport and he permitted me to enter Germany.

I ate a banana at the small bazaar within distance of the border. I returned ahead to Neumunster *via* Flensburg, Schleswig and Rendsburg.

At Bad Bremstedt I pitched my tent against the great hedge two yards off the main road and I gathered straw in the dusk for the tent floor before putting a reindeer fur rug and blankets on. I slept comfortably all that night.

* * * *

JULY 17. I discovered the tent and grass were completely damp when I came out of my tent in the dull morning.

At Hamburg many bricks have fallen down from the war-ruined buildings in the streets. It was the Royal Air Force's revenge in the Second World War.

Two Dutch cyclists from Amsterdam met me where I sat eating slices on the bank of the main road. They told me they were on their way to Copenhagen.

I passed Bremen on the River Weser to Delmenhorst.

About one mile off the south of Delmenhorst, I had to consider whether it would be wise to choose the new main road which I had never used before for the south. I continued into Weldeshausen where I saw the beautifully constructed barracks where the British soldiers are stationed. Numerous Dutch-styled German girls laughed at me when they spotted me, and I thought they were really silly. They are pretty young and healthy looking.

At the modern garage I was asked to enter the office where I had a friendly chat with a sympathetic German girl. I found her hospitable and kind.

I slept under my blankets on the pale yellowish grey weather-beaten and platformed hay in the warmth of the night air at the farm among the trees.

* * * *

JULY 18. I cycled southward to Nordhorn *via* Cloppenburg, Loningen, Daselunne and Lingen. At Lingen I wrote several postcards to personal friends of mine who live in Scotland and put them into the yellow post-box.

I arrived in Nordhorn which is a close neighbour to the German-Dutch border. The weather had been wet, but later only showery.

Concluding my complete tour at the German border entrance a German passport official passed my British passport and let me go to meet a Dutch passport soldier at the border entrance. Afterwards he permitted me to enter Holland.

Rammelbeek lies upon the Dutch-German frontier. Commencing a new tour, which may take me down to Arnhem *via* Oldenzaal, Hengelo, Lochem, Zutphen and Dieren to-day. Hengelo is a centre of the metal industry,

now being rebuilt in accordance with modern ideas after war-time devastation. Zutphen lies in one of the prettiest parts of rural Gelderland. In spite of war damage, this attractive old town with its ramparts and fortifications and narrow winding streets, still possesses many buildings which date from the Middle Ages.

I visited Zutphen on the River Yssel, one of the triplet sisters of the River Rhine. Nearing the conclusion of my tour at the north of Arnhem I pulled my tent out of the kitbag and cleared a pitch on the dry grass between the trees. There was no rain in the evening. I heard the noisy vibration of a train during my sleep in the tent.

*   *   *   *

JULY 19. Arnhem (population 160,000) earned unenviable fame as the scene of a great battle in September, 1944. It is situated on the River Lek. I passed Arnhem, a well-built town, to Nijmegen. Nijmegen (population 113,000), the city of Charlemagne, suffered considerable destruction during the Second World War, but the vitally important Waal Bridge was saved for the Allies. As is to be expected of a frontier stronghold which has existed since Roman times, Nijmegen has many old buildings; the oldest is the Valkhof, a ruined castle (with chapel) built by the Emperor Charlemagne about A.D. 800.

The great Rhine sweeps its waters westwards to the Swiss corner of Basel, and in turn still carries on northwards to the West of the Netherlands, where she divides her waters into the Dutch triplet rivers, Vaal, Lek and Yssel which run towards the openings of the North Sea from Lake Bodensee.

I visited Lake Bodensee in 1950 when I was in Austria.

196

In the task of eradicating the effects of the war period on the morals of the child, Holland has one advantage over some of its neighbours: it is still a Christian country. To see the crowd issuing from church at the end of a service is to realise that you are among a people to whom Sunday is more than the weekly holiday—it is still the day of the Lord.

I passed the mighty bridge across the River Vaal to land on the plain. Nijmegen lies on the River Vaal, I planned in my long travel to stop at the Dutch Belgian frontier *via* Graves, Hertogenbosch, Tilburg and Goirle.

Hertogenbosch, also known as " Bois-le-Duc" (population 54,000) is commercially important too; its history covers a much longer period. The great Cathedral of St. John (15th century) is a marvellous example of the flamboyant Gothic style.

Now I am at the frontier; traffic between the Dutch and Belgian zones is strictly controlled, but I do not understand why the two Dutch and Belgian passport officials allowed me to go on to Belgium without having examined my British passport; perhaps it was because I was a touring cyclist and not a driver of a car.

It was easy work cycling to Antwerp *via* Turnbout and Ostmalle. The origin of the name "Andhunerbo" in mediaeval Latin, or "Antwerpen " in Flemish, i.e., the place of hand-throwing, lies in the fact that cut off hands were thrown into the river. On the arms of the city to this day appear the castle and two severed hands.

* * * *

JULY 20. I followed the same main road to Ghent *via* St. Nicholas this morning. After my arrival in Ghent, I took appropriate

enough

the precaution of by-passing the local traffic to visit my old friend's home. I had a good hot bath before coming downstairs to the dining room, where I enjoyed a good dinner. The Flemings (Belgians) speak Flemish, which is low German practically identical with Dutch. They choose as their motto the Flemish sentence—"De taal is gansch het volk" signifying "The language is the whole people" which is appropriate enough.

After two o'clock I left Ghent for Bruges. I followed the important canal to Bruges *via* Eccloo and Maldegem. I found many delightful contrasts in the old town of Bruges. This is known as "Venice of the North."

Leaving Bruges after one hour, I arrived in Blankenberghe to find thousands of joyful holiday makers on the fine golden coast. I think Blankenberghe must be the most beautiful and greatest sea side resort on the European coast. Palatial hotels, villas and shops border the broad, handsome promenade looking out to sea.

I enjoyed a good walk along the lengthy seaside when the sun was shining warm upon me in the coolness of the windy air. The weather has been so fine and good. A man worked a dummy Punch with his hands inside the open-air small theatre. It was a first class show.

I am proud of being a visitor to Blankenburghe. I travelled southwards along the beautiful coast to Ostend *via* Wenduyne and Le Coq. I found many beautiful bungalows along the coast facing the sandy, grassy ground and the North Sea.

At Ostend I placed my tent upon the ground beside the empty sea-shore and slept overnight. I saw the towers floodlit far off from where I stood in the darkness of night.

* * * *

JULY 21. To-day Ostend is an even brighter place than it was in pre-war days. I am making my way in stages homewards to La Panne *via* Middelkerke, Westnde, Nieuport, Ooost-Dunkerke and Coxyde. At La Panne I saw a stout Belgian police man in white uniform with a white helmet.

At the Belgian-French frontier a French passport officer, like the Belgian, handed me my British passport back having stamped the date in my visa, as he granted me permission to enter France.

I visited the first French town, which is Dunkirk, with its war ruins. I remember thinking as I sadly looked at that French coast, of how my first cousin Mr. George Tait had been cruelly killed and drowned by the Germans in the Second World War. In my personal opinion, it would be difficult to find the spot where his bones are hidden in the bottom of the Straits of Dover, or removed into the deep. In fact, no human can tell, but the Lord alone knows best. In the pre-war days he was employed as a village cobbler, and was a good soccer player in the local junior team in Scotland. I still remember the picture of his face in my mind.

Leaving Dunkirk for Calais, I saw the lovely scenery with French farmhouses and church and trees far off. Fortunately I reached Calais in time to catch the steamer which was sailing in a few minutes out of the French seaport.

I crossed the Straits of Dover to Dover. A French passport mariner stamped the mark of departure date in the ninth visa of my British passport before I entered the steamer. I saw these tall white cliffs drawing nearer as we approached the shores of England.

At Dover an English passport official permitted me to

THE SCOTTISH TOURIST B

HASTE YE BAC
TO SCOTLAN

land after having examined my passport. I sensed at once that this is still the great English soil.

Happily I was ready to cycle up and down the rough and steep hills to Ashford *via* Folkestone, New Inn Green and Sellinge. After passing Ashford, I slept overnight in my tent in a field.

* * * *

JULY 22. I went back up to Wrotham Neath *via* Charing and Maidstone. At Wrotham Neath I turned left on another road to Oxtea *via* Lytham, Rivermead, Westerham and Limpsfield. At Oxted I visited the English bungalow, where I dined with Mr. and Mrs. Robinson. They are Christian Brethren by religion. He asked me what I thought of Oxted. I replied that it is a hilly village.

In the afternoon the lightning and the heavy rain lasted for almost three hours. I went out of the bungalow when the weather became clear and rainless.

I left Oxted for London, the British capital, where I stayed overnight.

At London I attended the evening service at the Apostolic Church.

* * * *

JULY 23. I am still in the city. Inside St. Paul's Cathedral I happened to find Miss Margaret Stewart, of Aberdeen, and her deaf mute boy friend from Edinburgh, where they were looking up at the marvellous and great memorials of many famous men. She is a daughter of an Aberdonian school-teacher. She said to me: "It is wonderful to have met you among millions of Londoners and visitors from all over the world."

204

I saw the beautiful memorial of Lord Kitchener, which is wholly made of white marble. His sleeping body lies in the uniform of a British Field Marshal. He was a hardy commander in the First World War.

At the Old Bailey I asked a smart barrister to guide me to see Lord Goddard, the Lord Chief Justice in the lengthy lobby. Afterwards he politely invited me to open the door and enter the Supreme Court.

I sat down, in interest, to see Lord Goddard, who sat watching the guilty lady amongst the barristers. The Royal Arms of timber are hung up above Lord Goddard's seat.

I was concentrating carefully to get clear of the dangerous London traffic at the opening of the northern plain a few miles off the crazy and busy city.

I set out for Luton *via* St. Albans which is the ancient town of Verulamium, which was founded soon after the Roman-conquest of A.D. 43. St. Albans Cathedral is one of the earliest Norman churches in England and possesses the longest Gothic nave in existence. At Luton I was allowed to sleep in the modern English prison for one night, because it was still raining. It would not be good enough to put up my tent on the wet grass under the evening rain. The prison is better than nothing.

*   *   *   *

JULY 24. Another police constable on day duty ordered me to get out at the front door after being dressed at six o'clock in the morning. But one of these police constables heartily engaged in a good chat with me.

The English people are chiefly descendants of the Angles and the Saxons, who crossed the North Sea from

Dummy Jim Film Made

Soundtrack Recorded

Alt W

dummyjim.com

Pitch at Cinemart

NOBO

IONA
BOOK
SHOP

Mother finds
Journal

Posts to Son

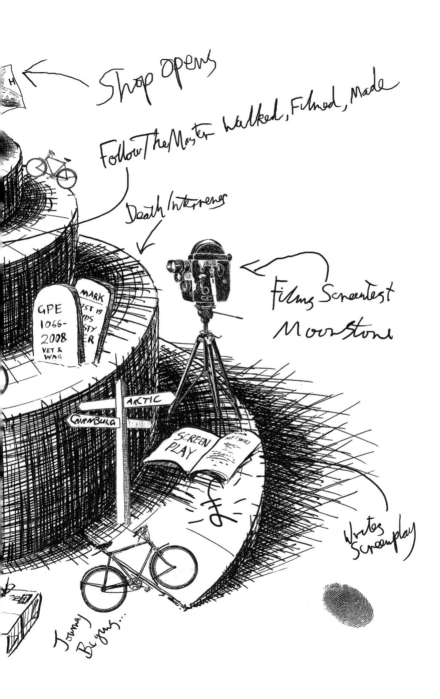

Shop opens

FollowTheMaster Walked, Filmed, Made

Death Intervenes

Films ScreenTest Moonstone

GPE
1066-
2008
VET &
WAG

MARK
~ST IS
~DS
~STY
~ER

ARCTIC

GRIMSBURG

SCREEN
PLAY

Writes Screenplay

Journey Begins...

Germany, "Deutschland," in the fifth and sixth centuries, and of a Norman-French element in the eleventh.

It was hard work setting out to Derby *via* Bedford, Kettering, Rothwell, Market Harborough, Leicester, Loughborough and Keyworth.

* * * *

JULY 25. I departed to Bolton *via* Matlock, Stockport, Manchester and Plendlebury. At Bolton I paid a visit to the Deaf Institute. Overnight I slept somewhere between Preston and Bolton.

* * * *

JULY 26. I cycled northwards to Preston, and westwards to Blackpool *via* Kirkham. At Blackpool I enjoyed a good walk on the sands. It is my own idea that the English seaside resort of Blackpool may be known as "Blaken-berghe of the North."

I returned eastwards on another road to Garstang from Grasmere *via* Lancaster, Carnforth, Kendal, Windermere and Ambleside.

The northern English climate changed to rain and dullness and darkness during my run northwards to Windermere and Lancaster. The Cumberland Lakes, situated among the highest hills in England, are celebrated for their beautiful scenery. Windermere, the largest lake in England, covers an area of three square miles. I noticed that the black-headed rams with round horns were eating grass among the rocks: the white clouds very slowly pass the great hills of Grasmere near which I spent the night under the roof.

*   *   *   *

JULY 27. I set out to the Scottish zone *via* Keswick, Bothel and Carlisle. Keswick is famous for its Annual Church Convention.

I reached the Scottish border, where I was happy to see the mighty but humble Scottish people again. I am a Scotsman by birth. Bonnie Scotland!

After my arrival in Dumfries *via* Annan, two local lads accompanied me to visit St. Michael's church. On a pillar to the right on entering the Church is a brass tablet indicating the position of the pew once occupied by Robert Burns, the highly-famed Scottish poet, and I was interested to touch his favourite pew for one minute.

This Church is now worthy of its long and honourable past, and fit to face with confidence as long a future. Dumfries is a handsome town: it was in the chapel of a monastery in town that Comyn was slain by Robert the Bruce in 1306.

At Dumfries I was well looked after by Mrs. A. Davidson and her family in her good home for one night. Her two deaf mute daughters were educated with me at the same time at Donaldson's Hospital, Edinburgh (now Donaldson's School for the Deaf). In fact I am not so proud of my old school, because I had never been encouraged to seek higher education. I found myself disappointed when I left school at sixteen. I held no higher leaving certificate. What a pity!

*   *   *   *

JULY 28. Leaving Dumfries, I arrived at Kilwinning *via* Thornhill, Sanquhar, Cumnock, Kilmarnock and Irvine.

As you make your bed,

so must you lie in it

At Kilwinning I accepted a kind invitation to reside in the home of my old schoolmate for one night.

* * * *

JULY 29. I travelled northwards to Gourock *via* Largs and Wemyss Bay, across the Firth of Clyde to Dunoon, on to Sandbank, where I sojourned over night at the home of Mr. and Mrs. Alex Stephen. He is a first cousin of mine on the side of my mother's people. He has been living and working in America for many years. He is a typical Scottish fisherman.

* * * *

JULY 30. In the morning I cycled back to Dunoon, across the Firth of Clyde to Gourock, on to Glasgow *via* Port Glasgow and Clydebank.

At Glasgow I slept calmly in my tent on the wasteful and fenceless field beside the great high wall of the famous Partick Thistle's Football Club.

The great city of Glasgow in Scotland is nationally celebrated for its engine making, steamship building and train building, which are the most important in the world. It has made three famous liners—Queen Mary, Queen Elizabeth and Carone—and many famous trains—The Royal Scot, etc. It is no less important for its varied and extensive manufacturers and commerce. It has a noble cathedral and university founded in 1450. The good, jolly and hospitable Glasgow citizens cry "Long Live Scotland For Ever." Without Glasgow Scotland would perish. Paisley is close to the city of Glasgow.

* * * *

JULY 31. In Maryhill, Glasgow, I paid a visit to the shoecraft repairs factory, where I greeted a number of deaf mute shoe-repairers. and Government trainees. Leaving Glasgow, it was my duty to go home to reach Falkirk *via* Stirling and Denny. At Falkirk I visited the home of Mr. and Mrs. Robert Waters. His red-haired wife was formerly Miss Jessie Buchan. They are both deaf and dumb. She belongs to the fishing village among the hills of St. Combs near Cairnbulg.

Falkirk is celebrated for its battles—the one in 1298, when Edward the First of England defeated the Scots under Wallace; the other gained by the Pretender in 1746.

At Grangemouth near Falkirk I visited the home of Mrs. Robert Waters' parents. Modern Scots are descended from a Celtic race which migrated from Ireland. Before the conclusion of the fifth century Old Scotland was known as "Scotia."

Carl Jacobsen said to his two Danish sons in the Danish Foreign Office Journal: "In Scotland you will find young men of good type; follow their example. The Scots are cheerful, natural, and stout-hearted; better and truer friends it would be hard to find."

I could agree with him in truth. My word proves nothing, but I confess my experience proves much.

I set out for a hilly field near South Queensferry, where I closed my eyes in sleep in my tent.

For the stronger we our houses do build,

The less chance we have of being killed.

August, 1951

AUGUST 1. I travelled by boat across the Firth of Forth past the Forth Bridge to North Queensferry. After landing at North Queensferry I began my travel to Newport in the direction of Burntisland, Kirkcaldy and Cupar. At Newport I crossed the Firth of Tay to Dundee where I paid a visit to the church and Institute for Deaf and Dumb Adults, where I had a personal talk with the Reverend William H. Wood (formerly a missioner of the Aberdeen Deaf and Dumb Benevolent Society), in his secretarial office. He had once come over to visit me in Cairnbulg when I was a little lad.

After an hour I departed to Montrose, *via* Arbroath and Inverkeilor. I arrived in the finely situated and handsome town of Montrose on my way home to Aberdeen. Though I visited the home of my deaf mute friends in town I also always love to see the airy, clean town of Montrose with its steeple and bridge.

In 1685 an English warrior wrote that Montrose was "a beauty that lies concealed, as it were, in the bosom of Scotland—most delicately dressed up." And a century earlier still, a French warrior recorded in his war diary that it was "a beautiful town." A beautiful town it is to this day, in its setting and in itself.

The earliest description of all was written in 1296, when John Balliol surrendered the throne of Scotland at Stracathro, only a few miles away. Edward the First of England, the Hammer of the Scots, chose Montrose as his headquarters on that occasion and his annalist made a note in-his diary that even in those remote times Montrose

216

was "a good town." I slept in my tent somewhere between Montrose and Inverbervie that night.

* * * *

AUGUST 2. It was hard work cycling to Aberdeen, known as "Granite City" and "Silver City" *via* Stonehaven from Inverbervie. I arrived in Aberdeen, where I shopped and rested part of a day, and stayed overnight.

* * * *

AUGUST 3. I left Aberdeen for Cairbulg, my homeplace *via* Ellon, Mintlaw and Lonmay.

At Schoolhill, Lonmay, I visited the home of Mr. and Mrs. Alexander Bruce. His mother, of remarkable and sympathetic intentions, was a real sister to my father. She was a good woman. She died a few years ago.

Once again the yawl fisherman greeted me as he was leaving his boat at the same time as I started my trip to the Continent last May 7th.

I arrived in Cairnbulg to stay in my own home again, thus concluding my great journey through Europe to the Arctic Circle.

APPENDICES

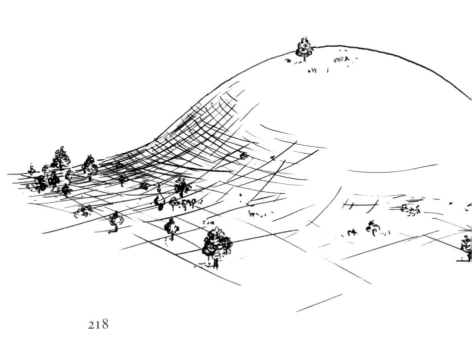

Even God cannot make two

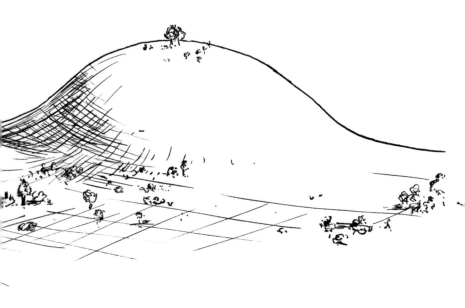

tains without a valley between.

FILM LINES
On Making, Doing and Making Do in *Dummy Jim*

Amanda Game

O wad some Pow'r the giftie gie us
To see oursels as ithers see us![1]

The movie camera has perhaps made Burns' dream of other sight come true.

Hulse's deft adaptation of the eccentric 1950's memoir, *I Cycled Into The Arctic Circle* by profoundly deaf Aberdonian James Duthie makes full use of the movie camera's potential to see otherwise and other ways. The film explores the tale of a maverick soul making a journey by bicycle through Europe in 1951: setting out for Morocco and ending up, in fact, several hundred miles above the Arctic Circle.

Deaf actor Samuel Dore takes the lead. His natural voice, articulating Duthie's thoughts and recollections, bears all the sound world of the deaf speaking: rough, strange, guttural. The subtitles exist not only for those who cannot hear but also for those who can hear perfectly well, but perhaps don't always listen.

A quotation threaded into the film – 'Language is the whole people' – gives pause for thought.

Interwoven with Dore / Duthie's filmed adventures by bicycle are collages of postcard-sized stills of place: church spires; birds; sentry boxes; flags, heather; hills; trees. Each clutch of postcards hints at images of national identity – random clichés perhaps but oddly telling. To see ourselves as others see us through images that we use to show ourselves to others: heather and hills for Scotland of course; coffee for Sweden; trees for Norway.

Stereotypes, archetypes: who is the stranger here? This is a film in which the camera is used to expose what the camera does: a process of probing what we see, how others see; how we see one another and the things around us.

This focus on the craft of film making is echoed in the crafting of other things shown: the knitting of jumpers; the drawing of illustrations for stop-frame animations; the cutting of granite and gravestone epitaphs; the pitching of a tent; kneading bread; sewing. We are drawn into the process, through the camera and the director's curious eye: the film is open source on a field of making.

Hands are in close up throughout. In one sequence, the camera lingers on a ball of wool threading up to dancing needles. We see the knitter, Jeni Reid, mark up another row finished: a form of notation like musical staves.

Early in the film, artist AnneMarie Walsh is observed creating sequential drawings that – once animated – are revealed as a cartoon depiction of Samuel Dore constructing and erecting the film's title out of plywood. Stylistically the lettering mimics the iconic Hollywood sign, a bold, clear statement: DUMMY JIM (*we made this ourselves, with our own hands*).

Another motif is the intimately shot hand – that of the film's editor Nick Currey – drawing with an ink pen: tracing routes, outlining landscape, adding handwritten quotes, making unforced errors.

The probing lens positions our hands with the knitter, the carver, the kneader and the draughtsman. Susan Sontag noted that in the early days of cinema, those watching were infused with "*a sense of wonder that reality could be transcribed with such immediacy*".[2] In *Dummy Jim* our sense of wonder is restored, despite our image saturated 21st century eyes.

That restoration is, in part, crafted for us by Hulse's focus on the making of things. This isn't the self conscious style seen in the BBC / V&A series 'Handmade in Britain', where certain kinds of process and skill are staged as a kind of symbolic ritual, distanced from everyday life and observed as historical curiosities. This is making and making do in everyday life today.

When the film shows knitter Jeni Reid fit Dore for a blue sleeveless pullover, we witness intimate judgments of care that making things brings: getting the right fit, stitch and tensions and of course the right colour – *blue brings out the colour of my eyes* approves Dore.

Reid's attention falters however under the eye of the camera: she knits up rather than casting off. The filmmakers – observing the scene – changed the making, just a little: we feel participant in and somewhat responsible for her uncertainty.

Judgments of care are, in part, questions of time: how we spend it, how we share it; how we experience it through other eyes.

Filmmaking's great capacity is to help us focus, to slow us down in order that we may see and feel the moments passing. In this respect film has synergy with other forms of making and taking time.

The camera pauses us, zooms us in, traces the typesetter's movements across the granite block; catches the flick of a bird across the sea; makes us wait in Duthie's empty single bedroom.

Each shot calibrates our sense of time in new ways: we enter another's life; another's experience through the stitching of jumpers; the hammering of tent pegs; the tracing of metal stencils on granite; the tightening of saddlebags.

Senses are heightened through the touch of the camera. Intricate details allow us to experience a sensuous material world: a cat's ear twitching, each hair moving to sound; a bee exploring the desiccated seed head of a sunflower; Magnus (the knitter's cat) warm and cozy against brightly knitted woolen squares of a blanket; the prick of a needle in the clumsy cyclist's thumb.

Dummy Jim does not tip into sentimentality however. The film language is precise, complex and pragmatic. Hulse keeps a sharp Brechtian focus. We watch as the past and the present merge. Narrative continuities meet disruptive discontinuities, techniques that give us agency to reflect upon the making of our own lives.

The fourth wall is removed early on when the present-day, undisguised Invercairn village hall features as a setting for Dore as he takes on the character of Duthie and sets off on his journey.

Local schoolchildren read aloud from the long-deceased cyclist's book, their rich Aberdeenshire vowels lending context and a sense of place to Duthie's musings.

Brecht lurks in the discontinuity: *Art is not a mirror with which to reflect reality but a hammer with which to shape it.*

The shots of cutting, lifting and shaping stone appear like interludes throughout the film: a glimpse of metal lettering gives a hint of the task at hand, but it is never explained, only shown.

Then, in a final moment of revelation, we see stonemasons drilling and fixing a memorial headstone to James Duthie in Invercairn cemetery: a stone that his family, like so many, could not afford to create when he died.

This is a moving moment, when we are all remembered by that act of remembering: of that careful crafting of our names on the hard, lasting stone.

The film's pitch perfect timing reminds us to see others as we see ourselves: the centre each of our own particular and remembered lives.

1. Lines from Robert Burns' poem 'To a Louse'.
2. p.188 Susan Sontag *A Century of Cinema* from *Where the Stress Falls* (*a collection of essays*).

Amanda Game is a freelance exhibition maker and producer. For thirty years she has worked in both museums and independent galleries, developing close collaborations with artists and designers who make everything from jewels to tableware to paintings as a way of exploring the wonders of their, and human imagination.

SENSING THE FILM
Phenomenology and Dummy Jim

Sarah McIntosh

From the opening scenes, the sense of texture in *Dummy Jim* is striking.

Walking through an abandoned, post-celebration village hall, we closely follow the character Jim (or is it the actor Samuel?) as he explores his environment in a particularly tactile way: picking up objects around him; pinching food off half-finished plates, pocketing biscuits, rifling through film props and cautiously trying on a woman's coat and hat.

As the film progresses, the use of differently textured film stocks and screen ratios add to a powerful, growing sense of haptic visuality.[1]

Dummy Jim is a man who cannot hear nor – in a conventional sense – speak. He experiences the world through a different balance and prism of senses. To better articulate this difference from what most of experience as reality, the film explores unconventional film language and unusual techniques.

Whilst much of contemporary film theory holds the sense of sight above all else, *Dummy Jim* can be seen as an example of phenomenological filmmaking, a film theory that gives holistic importance to all our senses in the experience of film viewing.

Phenomenological filmmaking takes a philosophical tenet at the heart of existentialism - *I think, therefore I am* – then inverts it: *I am, therefore I think.*

Instead of thinking of film in terms of being viewed passively, translated by the brain and then experienced by the body, phenomenological filmmaking looks at film as being experienced by the body first then interpreted and understood by the brain. More simply, it is our senses that inform our brain rather than our brain informing our bodies on how to react. This theory posits that film can be felt (or smelled or tasted) as much as it can be seen or heard.

Prioritizing materiality over representation, some films more than

224

others suggest this sense of embodiment in a heightened fashion.

Due to its close association with the sense of touch, one motif that occurs often in films linked with phenomenology and this particular type of filmmaking are images of hands. Extreme close ups of hands encourage the viewer to identify with them as if they were their own. The creation of a sense of touch relies on this identification and with our own sense of memory.

Therefore, when in *Dummy Jim's* opening sequence we see the two hands carefully sharpening a pencil with a scalpel, we are at some level identifying ourselves with those hands and remembering what it feels like to carry out the action ourselves. This disembodied image in fact makes us more aware of our own bodies. The motif is intensified when it is noted that the subsequent drawings witnessed are actually also hands, in this case hands that are hammering nails roughly into wood with a hammer.

Later on in the film we have several other examples of extreme close-ups of hands engaged in sensory, physical activity: flour-covered French baker's hands kneading dough; the nimble, cat-scratched hands of the female knitter and of course the hands of Jim himself, most notably when sewing on badges at his campsite.

But this evocation of sensorial memory is achieved not just through extreme close-ups of human hands; there are close ups of objects and animals that achieve the same outcome.

The uncomfortable proximity of image of the stonemason's grinder alongside its amplified noise remind of a dentist's drill and put the teeth on edge; the sensation of splintered wood is felt in the mouth as the horse chews at a wooden fence post and the breath of cows can be felt as they puff and snort at the camera lens.

The structure of Dummy Jim is multi-layered.

Frame by frame we see animations being made and then we watch the animation itself unfold; parts of the film's behind-the-scenes production are included in the final film and footage of Duthie's modern day community is interwoven with his history.

This intertextuality creates a feeling of uncertainty of place and time. Hulse's refusal to rely upon the authoritative voices of backstory and scripted dialogue leaves us somewhat alone and – in a cinema – we are literally in the dark.

A consequence of this temporarily insecure state is that we are more vulnerable to – and less distracted from – the film's touch.

225

Categorizing *Dummy Jim* as an example of phenomenological film-making places it amongst a group of very esteemed, mostly female, filmmakers. Names often mentioned in the context of the phenomenological theory include Claire Denis[2], Jane Campion[3] and – I propose – Kelly Reichardt[4].

Think on Laure's hands under the running water in Denis' *Vendredi Soir*[5], the sun between the fingertips in an extreme close-up in Campion's *The Piano*[6] or the minimal amount of dialogue in pretty much any Reichardt film but particularly *Old Joy*[7] or *Wendy and Lucy*[8]. Hand motifs, extreme close-ups, exaggerated sound and minimal dialogue can all be evidenced in the works of these women, as well as in *Dummy Jim*.

Yet whilst viewing *Dummy Jim*, other possible female influences were noted. Is there a possible link between the kneading dough of the female baker in *Dummy Jim* and the kneading of meatloaf in Chantal Akerman's *Jeanne Dielman*?[9] What about the use of various film stocks and split-screen images, could this perhaps be the influence of Agnes Varda? (see *The Gleaners and I*.)[10]

Some of the 16mm and 8mm images in the split-screen sequences reminded of Marie Menken, not just in the free-form way in which the camera moves in many of her films but also the film's overall musicality.

Conventionally in film, image and dialogue set the pace, reinforced by the sound effects and nuanced by music. However in Menken's *Arabesque for Kenneth Anger*[11] or *Glimpse of the Garden*[12] – and also in *Dummy Jim* – the directors surrender the primacy of the visual to the influence of the soundtrack.

Though none of these women mentioned are necessarily closely associated with Hollywood blockbusters, they still run the gamut between operating solely as film artists and those who have been bestowed some modicum of mainstream success.

Similarly, it's not possible to fully categorize *Dummy Jim* as it straddles the worlds of film art, animation and mainstream film.

Dummy Jim demands a more holistic approach to the art of filmmaking just as phenomenological theory demands a more holistic approach to viewing.

I CYCLED INTO THE ARCTIC CIRCLE

1. Marks, L.U., 2002. *Touch: Sensuous Theory and Multisensory Media*, Minneapolis; University of Minnesota Press.
2. Newton, E., 2008. The phenomenology of desire: Claire Denis's Vendredi Soir (2002). Studies in French Cinema 01/2008; 8(1):17–28. Abstract only. Available through: Taylor & Francis Online [09/07/2015]
3. Sobchack, V., 2004. *Carnal Thoughts: Embodiment and Moving image culture*, Berkeley: University of California Press.
4. Screenwriter and film director working within American indie cinema.
5. *Vendredi Soir*. 2002. [DVD] Claire Denis. France: Canal+
6. *The Piano*. 1993. [DVD] Jane Campion. Australia: Australian Film Commission
7. *Old Joy*. 2006. [DVD] Kelly Reichardt. USA: Epicentre Films
8. *Wendy and Lucy*. 2008. [DVD] Kelly Reichardt. USA: Field Guide Films
9. *Jeanne Dielman, 23 Quai du Commerce, 1080 Bruxelles*. 1975. [DVD] Chantal Akerman. Belgium: Ministère de la Culture Française de Belgique.
10. *The Gleaners and I*. 2000 [DVD] Agnes Varda. France: Cine Tamaris
11. *Arabesque for Kenneth Anger*. 1961 [Film] Directed by Marie Menken. USA: Anthology Film Archive
12. *Glimpse of the Garden*. 1957 [Film] Directed by Marie Menken. USA: Anthology Film Archive

Sarah McIntosh is a Film Studies graduate from Anglia Ruskin University. She currently works as a film programmer for Cambridge Film Festival in the UK and is the founder of a short film night dedicated to the promotion of female filmmakers entitled *Reel Women*.

THE CYCLES OF THE TEXT

Chris Fujiwara

In adapting James Duthie's *I Cycled into the Arctic Circle* into the film *Dummy Jim*, and in republishing the book together with materials related to the film in this volume, Matt Hulse has carried out a complex meditation on the various forms in which Duthie's experience might be conveyed. By doing this, Hulse is not merely trying to furnish some palatably sophisticated form in which that experience – a deaf Scotsman's travels through northern Europe six years after the end of World War Two – would match the preconceptions and prejudices of today (whenever, and wherever, today might be).

Nor is Dummy Jim another predictable exercise in self-reflexively meditating on the cinema, even though to indulge in such a meditation on this occasion would be more justifiable than usual, since Duthie is a remarkably cinematic figure. His bicycle trip re-activates a good part of the logic of cinema as it developed through the mid-20th century, as a machine based on cyclical motion, a device for capturing images of foreign lands, and a medium for commentary and instruction. Furthermore, as a deaf man, he threatens the conventional relationship of film to sound and language (film has often been drawn to the blind, but it is less comfortable with the deaf, Nicolas Philibert's In the Land of the Deaf being a beautiful recent exception).

Hulse is interested in Duthie's text as a series of encounters at the limits of language with European history and geography. Throughout Dummy Jim, Duthie's journey becomes written over by a proliferation of signs, representing the different ways people have of annotating their place in history: through music and song, through reading, writing, and reciting, through knitting, drawing, engraving, kneading bread… The artisanal intensity of the film (to which Amanda Game and Sarah McIntosh pay appropriate tribute in their essays in this volume) is a way of respecting this dimension of life, acknowledging that as we move around or stay at home, observing the changes in things around us and going through changes ourselves, we make everything into text.

So, in his text, Duthie knits together what he knows: his personal and family history, the history of his community and of the Scottish people, the histories of the places where he stops on his journey. Though a great task, it is small enough for him to make his own; he finds and describes a world to his size, one that is prepared to meet him and accommodate him. It is amazing to read how easily he makes friends wherever he goes, both among people who are deaf like him and people who are not.

In an e-mail to a teacher of deaf students, reproduced in this book, Hulse praises Duthie as "a great communicator." It's easy to see how Duthie's adventure might have been filmed as the heroic account of a triumphant success of communication, showing this "brave and intelligent man" (in Hulse's words again) undertaking an arduous journey across which he, overcoming the disadvantages of his deafness, affirms the common humanity of the European people at a time when the continent is still reeling from the cataclysms of war. It all seems to lend itself to what Hulse calls, in another e-mail, "the Hollywood treatment." Instead, Hulse keeps the euphoric temptation of Duthie's story at arm's length. Dummy Jim ends up being frayed, pulled apart, splintered, a work that, refusing any fixed image of community or of the heroic individual who tests and proves it, even permits a doubt as to whether what passes between Duthie (as played by Samuel Dore) and the other characters should be considered communication at all, or merely the same "illusion of contact" he, Hulse, finds himself beguiled by (as he writes in a letter to his mother) in the age of Skype.

As seen by Hulse, Duthie becomes a resolutely unheroic and deeply ambivalent figure: a man who conquers his solitude only by seeing it reproduced everywhere he goes. As much as he represents a triumph of communication (a triumph that it is still possible, in spite of everything, to be moved by), he also represents the failure of communication. This failure becomes inscribed in the film most interestingly through the figure of Monique, a pretty young baker Duthie meets in Charente, France, and who returns at various times in the film as both an obsessive erotic image and as a counter-narrator to Duthie, telling of the world she knows, which is held together by the giving and receiving of food. Monique's role has been greatly expanded from Duthie's book, in which she is a "charming young woman with colourful blue eyes" who occupies the author's attention for one paragraph and plays no further part in his recollections. In *Dummy Jim*, she acquires a name, parents, and an outlook on life.

Monique's significance in the filmic restructuring of the story proves crucial. Almost the first thing the reader of *I Cycled into the Arctic Circle* notices is that the author/narrator's original intention was not at all to go into the Arctic Circle but rather, setting forth from Scotland, to reach Morocco by way of France and Spain. Duthie's journey becomes disrupted when, on his way through France, he determines his bicycle has a faulty screw. He has it replaced in Charente and continues on his way south to Angoulême, "where," he writes, "I happened to find the French screw faulty again. I was going straight to Spain for Morocco and was deeply disappointed as I lost a great deal of time." It is at this point that he reverses direction and heads northward, through Poitiers, Tours, and Paris. Near Paris, he manages to acquire a new screw that he deems reliable, but instead of resuming his southward course he decides to go to Belgium and the Netherlands. From Groningen he crosses the border into Germany; from there he proceeds to Denmark, then Sweden, where he finally crosses into the Arctic Circle.

What is the reason for the improvisatory change in Duthie's route? Duthie's own text is not explicit on this point. Perhaps it's not only because of the defective screw, or his longing for cooler climes, that Duthie stops short of completing his original intention of going to Morocco. As long as he is still in Europe, he can be sure of encountering people who share his religion and his culture, and he moves among places that mirror one another (Copenhagen, he notes, is called the "Paris of the North"; he reflects that Antwerp, said by the Belgians to be a city of snobs, must be the "Edinburgh of the South"). To have gone on to Morocco would have meant leaving Europe and risking contact with the colonized other – which Hulse, disrupting Duthie's narrative, introduces into the film, in images (at once fantasy and documentary) of a night market and a man playing a lute. Monique's apparition occurs in the context of these images. Her sensuality seems to act as a warning to Duthie, making him realize that he is going too far south and should turn back. After that, she continues to resurface in Dummy Jim as the image of a communion that he has already renounced.

Though *Dummy Jim* celebrates Duthie's life, the film also bids a wry farewell to the Europe that Duthie knew and imagined. Seen in one light, Duthie's story is an elegy for the European project, the knitting-together of an inert "dummy," the erection of a monument whose purpose is finally to stop the circulation of texts. This is why Hulse sets them in circulation again, never lets them stop circulating: the great enemy (of life, of cinema) is a fixed and inert signification, so Hulse multiplies everything, refusing to let the wheel of meaning land at any one spot.

A text is something that is exchanged, that is passed around in silence (as Lacan, recalling Mallarmé, said), that is forged, touched, taken, kept ... It is this physical quality, the quality of something that is handled, over and over, and gets worn down through the handling (the most haunting phrase of *Dummy Jim* is a proverb Duthie coins: "Better to wear out shoes than sheets"), that Hulse's film seeks to register, together with the sense that one's own history and the histories of one's ancestors come entrusted to us as physical objects we need to care for. As this volume documents, the film itself, this strange outgrowth of and meditation on Duthie's journey, has now become one of the texts whose destiny is to be passed around in silence, from screening to screening.

Chris Fujiwara is a film critic and programmer. He has written several books and numerous articles on cinema and has lectured on film aesthetics and film history at Tokyo University, Yale University, and elsewhere. From 2012 to 2014 he was Artistic Director of Edinburgh International Film Festival.

PRAISED BY THE MAPMAKERS
(for JD of Invercairn)

John Mackie

they draw us out
on ribboning roads
beneath inquisitive skies
sunsets like lava
and
joyful migrations of mind

out here The Gods
are nomads;
spin with the wheels
bid us on,
as eager as we are,
for the next unknown

you carry your own
familiar
compass, lode and cornerstone
since
this bond bursting breath of maps
could scatter Him

across all
the fleeting beauty
of the world

October 2015

SELECTED CORRESPONDENCE FROM MATT HULSE'S INBOX 2001–2015

Hello … Matt? I'm contacting you after hearing of your proposed film about James Duthie.[1] I am one of a clique of friends who have been aficionados of *I Cycled* ever since we discovered the book lying around in the Ullapool Fishermen's Mission in the late '70s. If you wanted a researcher, an interpreter of Duthie's epic account, my brother Hamish knows it from cover to cover. Duthie inspired my short story *Bicycle Dreams*. PS: if you want the film rights to my novel *Antichaos* I am prepared to negotiate reasonably. PPS: if you are not Matt Hulse please ignore.

1. Hulse was interviewed on BBC Radio Scotland's *The Brian Morton Show*.

It was very nice to meet you.[2] I hope you enjoyed *Chronic Embarrass-ment*.[3] I was quite interested in *I Cycled Into The Arctic Circle* as this is quite a large project to take on in terms of production values and I quite liked the simple, religious deaf man travelling to far places with a small mind of how people lived in their different cultures and trying his best to take it all in – tone.

Road movies can be hard to make and to be successful as they seem to be devoid of any plotting but I'm a huge fan of them as there's lots of character development, soul-searching elements, exploration of scrumptious landscapes and meeting a huge variety of characters. Witnessing a huge journey from start to end brings out the best in the audience as we finally reach the end of someone's huge journey for whatever reasons for its finish.

Immediately David Lynch's[4] *The Straight Story*[5] comes to mind as it has a few elements which is the same as *I Cycled* so if this film was made you'd be able to find an audience to watch it.

1. Graphic designer, film director, photographer and film critic who plays the lead in *Dummy Jim*.

2. Hulse attended Wolverhampton's *Deaf Film and Television Festival* (now *Deaffest*) and was introduced to Dore by Lucy Franklin of the British Deaf Association.

3. Dore's short comedy charts the misfortunes of three enthusiastic deaf Bristolian clubbers.

4. American film director, television director, visual artist, musician, actor and author known for surreal films that "disturb, offend and mystify" audiences (Lynch and Rodley 2005. p.245)

5. 1999 biographical drama film edited and produced by Mary Sweeney, Lynch's partner and co-worker. The film is based on the true story of Alvin Straight's 1994 journey across Iowa and Wisconsin on a lawn mower.

01.02.10 15:41h   Subject: Onwards!   From: Matt Hulse

Dear Sam, To give Dummy Jim the Hollywood treatment – even a flavour of it – or worse a failed attempt at it – would be to deny the spirit of the book and James Duthie.

02.02.10 09:52h   Subject: Re: Onwards!   From: Samuel Dore

It's really interesting the new direction you're taking. Shame we aren't getting the chance to shoot the script you've always wanted but there's no reason why we shouldn't explore in new ways.

02.02.10 13:27h   Subject: Re: Onwards!   From: Matt Hulse

These are not new ways. Since Tishna[1] and I parted professional ways I have turned my back on the screenplay. The very concept of needing a screenplay to work from – following the conventional industry approach to financing – has been thrown in the bin. The bare bones remain useful but the fleshing out needs to happen in a more immediate, energetic, playful way.

The event we all took part in at the CCA[2] marked that new direction. (*I feel as if I am seeing history in the making* said a colleague afterwards).

Having completed a feature film,[3] I now realize that a lot of the 'fuss' around features is an illusion. In the end it boils down to single-mindedly piecing together footage in the way that one knows best, rather than changing the whole way one works (just) because it's a 'feature'.

1. Tishna Molla, *Dummy Jim*'s original sole producer (later co-producer), attached to the project through film production company Tall Stories (London). Several years into development Molla called Hulse. Molla: *I don't think I can produce this film.* Hulse: *Well I don't think I can direct it.*

2. The new website *dummyjim.com* was launched at Glasgow's Centre for Contemporary Art on 23rd August 2008, and featured a live performance by The One Ensemble (joint composers of the film's score), readings from Duthie's journal by Marie Denarnaud (French actress who plays Monique in the film) and a public plea for sponsorship from Hulse. The first donation in support of the new fund-raising strategy emerged that night from Darri Donnelly and Tamara van Strijthem in the form of a Scottish £20 note stuck into an empty (miniature) bottle of Scotch.

3. Hulse's debut feature-length film – *Follow The Master* – a documentary following the film maker, his girlfriend Lucy Brown and dog Tippy on a 100 mile long walk of The South Downs Way, a journey made in tribute the Hulse's recently deceased grandfather, Eric.

03.02.10 10:47h   Subject: Re: Onwards!   From: Samuel Dore

You are going to tackle the film in a kind of homemade way: a touch of Duthie. He was a soldier, doing what he wanted to do and not worrying about the consequences. That's what you're going to do too – and we all know it will turn out the way it was supposed to be.

21.02.10 04:25h   Subject: Quality or Merit   From: Matt Hulse

Thank you for looking at my film *Follow The Master*. Unfortunately the festival that you run in order to show case eccentric & personal work has not, on this occasion, risen to the challenge.[1]

This does not mean that your festival has neither quality nor merit. My films are extremely unusual and *Follow The Master* is no exception. Dare I suggest that you have lost some of that essential DIY freewheeling vision that I associate with AAFF? This year you received 2,500 submissions from 67 countries. One simply cannot program films on a corporate scale and maintain quality.

Although your festival has fallen short this year, I hope that you will continue to care passionately about the art of film and seek out my work in future. That's if you can find the time, whilst you paddle to stay afloat in that tsunami of well-heeled flash young guns with well-oiled distribution networks behind them.

Again, thank you for valuing my work by using the DVD screener as a drinks coaster. No, really: please recycle.

1. Hulse's email to the Ann Arbor Film Festival closely mimics the tone and wording of the standard rejection email he had received from them.

10.08.10 11:45 h   Subject: Re: Lunchbreath Design Fantasy
                    From: Matt Hulse

When Olly & Alex did their trip[1], I asked them to take photos of where their tent had been set up, ie the patches of flattened grass, with a view that these could have been Duthie's, but also as a record of their own journey – *the making of a lasting impression.* This is actually PreDR[2]. I'd like to use these for a set of postcards, with the addition of your hand-written text, you know: *Örnsköldsvik, dusk, 15th June, 1951.*

1. In the summer of 2010, musicians Alex South and Olly Rundell made a spon-
   sored cycling trip from Glasgow to the Nordkapp (Norway), following a route
   similar to that taken by James Duthie in 1951. Duthie failed to reach Nordkapp,
   but South and Rundell were successful, raising over £2000 each for *Dummy
   Jim* and the UK charity *National Deaf Children's Society.*
2. *Post-design rationalization* (PDR) describes the process of justification resort-
   ed to when explaining the thinking behind (completed) work that fails to turn
   out as originally intended. Arguably most creative practice is the result of trial
   and error, discovery and improvisation, although artists in particular – and the
   gallery system that supports them – would prefer that a maker be portrayed
   (and therefore remembered) as a genius that knew what they were doing all
   along. Hulse and Currey often accuse one another of *PDR*. The underlying fear
   is that the pair may not be fully in control of their work. By invoking *PreDR*
   Hulse is appealing to Currey that he'd thought the plan through from start to
   finish.

10.08.10 13:11 h   Subject: Re: Lunchbreath Design Fantasy
                    From: Nick Currey

Patches of damp grass might look fascinating to us, but a non-arty GUNT[3] may disagree! They look very bleak to me. The colour images are less bleak, in fact they look like old '50s printed postcards – John Hinde[4] heightened colours plus a sad, blue-ish tinge. It's amazing we have girlfriends.

3. *"The bulge created by lower abdominal fat ballooning out below the tight-
   ened waistband of a fat lady's pants, below the gut and just above the see-you-
   next-Tuesday."* – urbandictionary.com
4. English photographer, whose idealistic and nostalgic style influenced the art of
   postcard photography.

10.08.10 14:23h   Subject: Re: Lunchbreath Design Fantasy
             From: Matt Hulse

Duthie: a damp, austere, black and white man, supping cold soup and LIKING IT. Try and divert me from making the Great Bleak Art Movie with a Wry Hint of Humour and you will find yourself with an Angry Irish Fight[5]. Plus I have discovered that way back the Jumps (my descendants) were from what is now Poland. So I shall stare at you with an inscrutable Polish expression. And make you sup thin bleak gruel with a knob of lard in the shape of the Pope.

"It is in the eternal struggle between soup and bread that the meal is made."

5. When drunk, Currey resorts to calling Hulse (who is partially Irish) 'mad Irishman', particularly when the director is in danger of winning an argument through sheer force of conviction.

10.08.10 15:01h   Subject: Re: Lunchbreath Design Fantasy
             From: Nick Currey

You ask, so I tell, but in the end you must do what you like. I'm happy to be a sounding board to kick against and make your ideas resolve via thesis/antithesis/synthesis but if you don't want my opinion, de-loop me, Władysław! My God. You have Chopin[6], Górecki[7], Penderecki[8], Polanski[9] and Kieślowski[10] mixed in with Matthew Arnold[11]. Your black slotted spoon[12] is in the post: miserable gunt.

6. Polish composer and virtuoso pianist of the Romantic era.
7. Polish composer of contemporary classical music.
8. Polish composer and conductor. *Threnody to the Victims of Hiroshima* (1960) is amongst his best known work.
9. Naturalized-French/Polish film director, producer, writer, and actor.
10. Polish film director and screenwriter.
11. English poet and cultural critic. Hulse is named after him. Arnold is characterized as a sage writer – one who chastises and instructs the reader on contemporary social issues.
12. In 2009 Hulse was artist in residence at Wooda Farm (North Cornwall) where – with Currey's assistance – he edited his debut feature *Follow The Master*. He kept an online journal (blog). This entry is from 26th February 2009: *Anyway, this fine, sunny morning I'm here to share with you my thoughts about Death. It's an important subject and one that's been, unsurprisingly, uppermost in my mind since I've been working on this film about my deceased Grandpa, Eric. I've been going through some pretty dark times in my completely silent bedroom. I've not been scared, more awestruck. It feels as if Death has been*

lurking around a bit. For many years I've had a kind of 'standard' dream in which I awake suddenly, pulling myself away from Death's door – these feel like 'near-Death' experiences but are probably more to do with snoring or having had a curry that night. The main thing with these experiences is that I'm pulling myself back from some kind of brink. The difference now is that somewhere deep within my dreaming I've made a conscious decision to 'take on' the experience – you know: come on then Death, do your worst, let's see what really happens. Over the ages there have been wise sages and voyagers into the unknown. I can safely say that my name may now be added to those brave few who challenged Death to answer the question: Death, what are you? I got my answer the night before last – Death is a black slotted spoon. Surely anyone can accept that? Fear mortality no more, all it amounts to is a kitchen utensil. My dream also taught me one must ultimately go through the slots of the spoon. I'll figure that out when the time comes but I'll let you know if I work it out before the time. Death Makes Noodles of Us All. If the residency has led me to accept my own eventual and inevitable demise, then that alone is worth it? Next: Tarkovsky vs You've Been Framed.

10.08.10 23:17h   Subject: Re: Lunchbreath Design Fantasy
              From: Matt Hulse

I am getting auld and tired. Maybe an album, concerts, feature film, DVD, book, postcards, badges, website and a line of bespoke Dummy Jam[13] preserves is plenty to be getting on with. Someone suggested *Dummy Jim Jams* and at that point I realized a limit had been reached. Look. We'll make a nice product with quality, integrity and fun. They buy it. Simple. They don't even yet KNOW that they like images of absent tents – but they will.[14]

13. Designer/maker Evie Milo's handmade pots of jam.
14. Very few postcards were sold.

27.09.10 23:54h   Subject: Postcards!   From: Nick Currey

K[1] said I should tell you the dream I had last night. You and I were making a film together, staying in a sort of big, posh log cabin, with wallpaper and proper furniture. Anyway, prior to starting on the film we decided we HAD to write slogans all over all the surfaces of our dwelling, so not only walls but inside drawers, under tables etc. The slogans were revolutionary calls to action and artistic statements, as well as private confessions and enthusiasms. We were half way through the process when K woke me up.

1. Kerry Hopkins.

28.09.10 01:16h   Subject: Re: Postcards!   From: Matt Hulse

It's close to Reality. It's going in The Book. Did we use biros? I remember that Sad Puniness[2] from school, scratching away into smelly wood, then in later years failing to complete words on Formica surfaces.

I spoke to Eunice.[3] She said her Grandfather's sister had a lifelong limp after a certain James Duthie booted her in the leg. Initially I had a vision of him as an adult, in his suit and hat, kicking some poor wee child – but of course they were both kids at the time. She said it was because he was 'tormented'.

2. Kerry Hopkins and Lucy Brown visited Currey and Hulse in 2009 at Wooda Farm. A day trip to nearby Padstow is remembered by all as a desultory, rain-sodden, depressing affair. Hopkins' mobile phone – set to 'predictive text' – suggested *sadpuny* as an option for *Padstow* and it stuck.
3. Head teacher at Inverallochy School.

29.09.10 01:11h   Subject: Re: Postcards!   From: Nick Currey

We used marker pens as well as paintbrushes and black paint. I see that 'booting the girl thing' as a great dream sequence. Useful to add grit and show he's not just an obsessive saint. He could try and swat flies using exactly the same kicking action – little effect bringing him up short.

01.10.10 02:39h   Subject: Re: Postcards!   From: Matt Hulse

Duthies fatal road accident remains unexplained – apparently with 'no other vehicle involved'.[4] This seems odd, given that he made a 16,000 mile trip on the same scooter, across 18 countries (true story). I had a startlingly clear vision last night that this was caused by 'road bullying': he was forced to swerve. The drivers up there can be aggressive and flashy – a motor is a huge status thing. The Fraserburgh cemetery is dotted with young lads killed before they hit 21, with laser-etched photos of powerful cars on headstones.[5] The tormenting must surely have continued as all got older – with more powerful means to bully with.

4. *Cairnbulg World Traveller Dies After Accident*, Fraserburgh Herald, 18th June 1965.
5. Hulse later discovered that many of these young people in fact died during an epidemic of heroin abuse in the area.

01.10.10 03:38h   Subject: Re: Postcards!   From: Nick Currey

Your musing on Duthie's death reminds me of a recondite item that little

Andy[6] and I refer to in our occasional dealings. We say to each other, on bidding farewell: *Take the Wall.*

In the '30s to the '60s an anonymous correspondent on all matters motor biking went by the moniker of Ixion. In Greek mythology Ixion was bound to a burning wheel for all eternity. Andy told me once that in his monthly article, Ixion was discussing the Law of The Road, and ended by proposing a hypothetical situation, which went something like this (my words but you get the idea):

Dear reader and brother of The Road, if you happen to be away from the cares of everyday life, upon your metal mount and travelling at speed, and suddenly passers-by are before you, if only two options present themselves at that instant – to hit the passers-by or hit a wall and face certain death – then be the man and Take The Wall.

6. Andy Holmes, also known as *Little Andy*.

01.10.10 03:53h   Subject: Re: Postcards!   From: Matt Hulse

I would Take The Wall. Instinct. I might even do it if a sheep were astray on the road, if I had time. Nice thoughts, strangely reassuring. Perhaps Jim swerved to avoid Monique[7], who's walked barefoot from Paris, bearing a huge tart with the ornate, saucily impertinent icing inscription: *Prends La Mur!*

7. A character and suggested 'love interest' in *Dummy Jim*, played by Marie Denarnaud.

14.10.10 10:47h   Subject: Quick Fire Craziness   From: Matt Hulse

When I look at Duthie's text I think: *I can't do this.* It's really not me. It's actually negative. Not right. Essentially I am bored/tired of the 'job' of sorting all this out, of the process of completing this film, I want to be moving on to the next thing. Something needs to change – I think radically – to energize it.

There's a story to be made out of this material. I can be a director. But my heart/mind/life is moving on. After 10 years, that's not surprising. I feel as if I am wasting my time. What I really want and need to be doing is … swimming, activity, moving, making a film with Tippy, out in the forest, drumming up Mount Everest, taking Ruth[1] to New York, dancing with you – whatever.

What has excited me recently? Eunice's funny upturned impish face, twinkly, ready to make mischief. Joy's[2] funny jokes, Lorraine's[3] canny

241

asides – and how you and I have started to work together. All the odd connections I've made, the *Dummy Jim* concerts.[4] These seem to me to be the important things: they energize. I follow instinct … there's some-thing … not wrong … but misled? My dream scenario is … to pass the buck. That's what I am facing. Is it even possible to say that there is to be no film?

1. Ruth Pendragon, Matt Hulse's mother. It has been a dream of Pendragon's for several decades to visit New York, but cost and anxieties about flying have proved prohibitive.
2. Joy Buchan (née McLeman), one of James Duthie's second cousins – open-minded advocate and active supporter of the film throughout its development (see p.187).
3. Joy's daughter, Lorraine Buchan.
4. In November 2009 *The One Ensemble and Sarah Kenchington* premiered a suite of new works composed for *Dummy Jim* at live concerts across Scotland. Hulse projected clips of footage from the film-to-be, along with extracts from the screenplay and Duthie's journal. (See p.123)

16.10.10 05:57h   Subject: Re: Quick Fire Craziness
                  From: Lucy Brown

I don't think it's realistic to hope to feel really positive and inspired about the project all the time. You're bound to waver, and have doubts and concerns – especially after all this time, and when you're alone in a big house in the middle of nowhere drinking whisky and wine.[1]

I don't think you really want to give up on DJ, I just think you want to get on with other things, so let's get on and make the film. You've already got lots of great ideas. You can't quite figure out the whole thing yet, but SO WHAT. If you can imagine a few scenes that get you excited in themselves then let's just get on and film them, see what it looks like, play with Nick & Alan[2], make a book to put it in. THIS is your process, and the result is something none of us can yet know.

You've always spun magic Matt, but perhaps you haven't had to think about it so much before? Stop thinking, have fun with it.

1. Hulse isolated himself on the Isle of Skye to write and research.
2. Alan Brown. Artist, designer, creator of *dummyjim.com* and animated inter-ludes for *Dummy Jim*.

19.10.10 10:13h   Subject: Jan Van Os' Niece
                   From: Karen Van Os-Cassells

Uncle Jan[1] told me about your next project, *Dummy Jim*. I teach deaf/
hard of hearing students between the ages of 4 and 21 at Public Schools
in St. Paul, Minnesota. All my students are mainstreamed,[2] and all
schools are in an urban setting. The majority of my students are refu-
gees or immigrants. I see them one on one for primary instruction in
reading, writing, math, auditory functioning and compensation skills.
They are often the only person in their family or community with hearing
loss and so I love to share with them stories of inspirational deaf or hard
of hearing people. I think it's so very important for my students to know
that they can do anything their hearing peers can do – except hear, of
course. I am delighted that you have chosen to tell the story of a deaf
person. Our hearing society is not familiar with the rich history of Deaf
Culture and many hearing people still see deaf people as "dumb" or to
be pitied. Did you ever find out anything more about the mysterious
car accident that killed *Dummy Jim*? I know that'll be the first thing my
students will want to know :–)

1. During their 100 mile long walk of The South Downs Way in 2008, Lucy Brown
   and Matt Hulse met two Belgian walkers, Jan van Os and Nille Hannes. Van
   Os and Hannes appear in Hulse's debut feature *Follow The Master* as *Some
   Belgians* and reappear in *Dummy Jim* as *Antwerps*.
2. Deaf/hoh students are integrated with hearing peers.

19.10.10 10:13h   Subject: Re: Jan Van Os' Niece   From: Matt Hulse

I would be delighted if *Dummy Jim* can help in some way. Duthie was
a great communicator. He was a brave and intelligent man in a 1951
community that people there have described as 'brutal'. Would it be
helpful for you to have some *Dummy Jim* teaching materials? I could
send you (free of charge of course) a BSL finger-spelling tea towel[3],
'visiting' cards, perhaps a few button badges? Regarding the accident
– there is little information on that. It was a 'road accident' in as much
as it happened on a road, although reportedly no other vehicle was
involved. James was on a motor scooter, not a bicycle. You can imagine
that I have thought of all sorts of scenarios and how to show it in the
film. Or do I show it at all? It's sad that he was killed this way but at the
same time he was doing exactly what he loved – travelling.

2. To support Alex South and Olly Rundell's fundraising efforts during their

Glasgow-Nordkapp cycling trip, tea towels were produced (see p.45 and p.77). These were designed by Nick Currey, hand-printed by Fiona McIntosh (Tessuti, Scotland) and finished by Lucy Brown.

21.10.10 08:41h   Subject: Type   From: Matt Hulse

I know you loathe Facebook[1], but I consider myself a kind of trouble-maker between the obviously correct and the questionable. There's a role there and I am doing it. Punching within the envelope? Anyway, there's this little stupid thing where it says *Write Something About Yourself*, and I explore this constantly – actually, I see it as a commission – and here is my most recent effort, inspired in part by your work.

This bit, half cut
With few words
Free, roughly
True to type
Middling
Smaller
Matty
Matt
Me
I

1. Online social networking service headquartered in Menlo Park (CA) with over 1.18 billion monthly active users as of June 2015.

21.10.10 20:10h Subject: Re: Type From: Alice Smith[2]

That's bloody great that! You should stick it on a business card.
Dabbling in DaDa[3]. I get it about Facebook, everyone's transported their lives up there. We're trailing behind, and it's tempting, but I daren't, I'd never get back. Tell us – what it's like up there?

2. British illustrator who designed the cover of the book you are now reading. Along with her partner – typesetter Christian Brett – she helped Hulse complete this tome.
3. An art movement of the European avant-garde in the early 20th century. The Dadaists – "monteurs" (mechanics) – used scissors and glue rather than paintbrushes and paints to express their views of modern life through their reworking of images and texts presented by the media.

I CYCLED INTO THE ARCTIC CIRCLE

24.11.10 22:04h   Subject: Re: Type   From: Matt Hulse

I have been thinking about Mark's ashes[4], and how he hated going for walks. Sounds a little far-fetched and romanticized but something that feels right is to send him off in/as fireworks, with The Wedding Present[5] blasting out full volume. Mark had this volatile, unexpressed sense of violence, which he suppressed through drink and articulated through his painting. He was aware of this too; we discussed it at length. For several summers we went together to the *fiesta* in Bilbao[6] where they have these anarchic, lawless firework displays every night – which he adored. He also loved the immediate, instantaneous 'blasting/blowing out' of money – cash into explosions – what's money for anyway? Get rid of it as soon as possible. He loved/loathed 'safety' in equal measure. Fireworks articulate that. He liked the clean/neat distance of the violence – he didn't get his hands dirty and didn't need to walk very far to enjoy the effect.

It's a thought. It occurred to me when Lucy and I were in Malta[7], where they have nightly explosions. Unremittingly. We could create a few sparks up on the moors[8] maybe?

4. Mark Smith was Hulse's closest friend and confidant at the University of Reading where the pair studied Art between 1987–1991. Illustrator Alice Smith is Mark's niece. Following Mark's death in 2007, Hulse approached Alice to create the poster for his debut feature *Follow The Master*. Mark worked for a period at the ISBN Agency (London). In the days before it was possible simply to buy an ISBN number for a book, aspiring 'published authors' considered the 13-digit barcode a sign of validation; a book was not a *proper* book without one. Mark's job was to filter out the many amateur, self-published works that were submitted to the agency. Naughtily, he kept many of these books and would share these with Hulse, during end-of-the-working-week drinks in London's Soho. These works of unsophisticated genius – with titles such as *Saxophone of Death*, *RECIPE COOK BOOK by Madeline on Meals: For a more healthier way of life (see p.27)* and *A Tribute to Klaus Wünderlich* – remain the most well-thumbed in Hulse's modest library. One of these books, the pamphlet *Eight Passion Proteins With Care* by Stanley Green, features in *Dummy Jim*. Mark died in his sleep in Rochdale shortly after his 46th birthday, following years of serious depression, alcohol and drug abuse, creative insurgency, gentle mayhem and willful disobedience. Sadly perhaps, Mark never got to see *Dummy Jim* – although it's arguable he would have fallen asleep whilst watching it, and cleared the cinema with his infamous snoring or, more likely, he would have been propping up the bar. However, in recognition of its own brand of unsophisticated genius and in acknowledgement of Mark's deep

influence, an edition Duthie's book sits proudly alongside other volumes that Hulse received from his troublesome – and troubled – friend.

5. British indie rock group based in Leeds, England, formed in 1985 from the ashes of the *Lost Pandas*. Throughout their career they have been led by vocalist and guitarist David Gedge.

6. City in Spain; capital of Biscay in the autonomous community of the Basque Country.

7. A Southern European island country comprising an archipelago in the Mediterranean Sea.

8. Blackstone Edge, Saddleworth Moor and the South Pennines are close to the east of Rochdale.

27.10.10 22:36h   Subject: This Is A Film For Children
                   From: Matt Hulse

Dear Nick, Was interesting having Rob here[1]. He was disturbed by the fact that I shaved in the afternoon. Managed a bit of man-to-man about getting old/older. He said he felt inspired by how Lucy and I were 'so good at recycling our lives'. Not sure what to make of that.

My time in Skye was weird. But the pain will produce gain. I did need to take a brave and fresh look. One of the most illuminating moments was re-reading something I wrote back in 2003:

James was literal, not literary. It is his unique tone – rather than the text's meaning – that reveals his character, and it is this tone that is interesting and entertaining. My aim is not to mock but to articulate his specific quality of thought, turn of phrase, form of reasoning, without recourse to disembodied monologue/voice over.

A 'collagist' approach to film making has dictated the look and feel of much of my work. There's always been a close relationship between the method and the end result and I Cycled Into the Arctic Circle[2] will follow this precedent. I like to think of my films being constructed from a number of simultaneously unfolding 'tracks' – as viewer we are present- ed with the intersections and crossovers of these strands of image and sound.

We will (continue to) shoot and source a diversity of pertinent and inspiring material, building the film incrementally and thoughtfully, allowing the project to grow on a number of fronts simultaneously. I don't envisage the need for a single, extended, intense shoot, but rather a series of shorter, focused 'outings' that allow time and space for experiment, reflection and crucial on-going research and development.

246

I agree with myself. What I've had to do since the 'collapse' of the Tishna/Scottish Screen/UKFC model[3] is turn the boat around and get back to what I do best. That's where we're headed. I need to believe that the way I make films is RIGHT for this story. I must not feel that I am somehow doing it 'wrong', or 'weakly'. This is a genuine haunting fear.

1. Robert Trueman – aka *Canadian Rob* – close friend of both Hulse and Currey. Rob stayed with Matt Hulse, Lucy Brown and Tippy at the flat they shared in Edinburgh.
2. The original working title for what became *Dummy Jim*.
3. The original finance plan for the film was to involve several funding partners including Scottish Screen, UK Film Council and additional European co-production partners. Although this strategy raised awareness of the project and supported the development of the screenplay, after several years work – five at the very least – it did not lead directly to the film being financed.

02.11.10 20:53h   Subject: Picasso's Äventyr   From: Nick Currey

Thanks very much for *Picasso's Äventyr*.[1] A classic curate's egg of a film – there are too few of these about. It has some great surprises in it and some really bizarre subversive moments. It has a slightly flabby notion of comic timing (or maybe that is Swedish comic timing?). It reminded me less of Monty Python[2] than of Lindsey Anderson's[3] film *O Lucky Man!*[4] – another curate's egg – but without the bleakness and sting of cruelty that managed to make you feel unsettled and at sea. By the way – I asked before – what's this 'strongest suite' of mine you mentioned?

1. A 1978 Swedish comedy film directed by Tage Danielsson starring Gösta Ekman as the famous painter. The film uses ten languages: Spanish, French, Swedish, German, Finnish, Italian, English, Russian, Norwegian and Latin. Most of these words are very simple (*agua*, water), sometimes meaning something different from what they seem. Hulse originally received a copy of the film from his Swedish friends Malin Gezelius and Lena Karlsson, who make a fleeting appearance in *Dummy Jim* as *Happy Swedes*.
2. Monty Python (or *The Pythons*) were a British surreal comedy group who created the sketch comedy show *Monty Python's Flying Circus*, first aired on the BBC on 5 October 1969. The show was conceived, written and performed by its members Graham Chapman, John Cleese, Terry Gilliam, Eric Idle, Terry Jones, and Michael Palin.
3. British feature film, theatre and documentary director, film critic, and leading light of the mid-1950s Free Cinema movement and the British New Wave.
4. Surreal 1973 British comedy-drama fantasy film, intended as an allegory on life in a capitalist society. Anderson decided musician Alan Price should write the

score and sent him the script, indicating where he would like songs to appear. Price wrote nearly all the songs before filming started. Anderson conceived of Price's role as a kind of Greek Chorus, both commenting on and finally appearing as part of the action. Hulse followed this example, inviting *The One Ensemble and Sarah Kenchington* to compose music in advance of filming. Their 2009 soundtrack album preceded the completed film *Dummy Jim* by four years. *The One Ensemble and Sarah Kenchington* appear as part of the action in *Dummy Jim.*

02.11.10 06:54h   Subject: Re: Picasso's Äventyr   From: Matt Hulse
Strongest suite? Maybe I mean *strongest hand*? A combination of animation, documentary, drama-ish bits, surrealism, graphical eye, comedy, facts, sense of design, willingness to read the instructions, willingness to ignore the instructions, beer capacity, taking punches like a man.

06.01.11 23:01h   Subject: Dummy Dummy   From: Matt Hulse
Feeling very positive about DJ and all who sail inside. 2010 was the year that I turned the liner in the right direction and there's no stopping it now. Remember this: Titanic was built by professionals and the Ark by amateurs.

Regarding the notion of 'writing' with the edit. I would love you to come aboard as a co-writer, and for us to engage with that writing process fully, but through co-editing, if you see what I mean.

07.01.11 00:27h   Subject: Re: Dummy Dummy   From: Nick Currey
Are we the Titanic or the Ark? I'm happy to be regarded as co-writer certainly and am flattered etc. This sort of thing will become clear as the process goes on. And we certainly needn't get too worried about credits at this stage. (Mind you, maybe 'Guest'[1] won't cut it credit-wise …) I'll let you know when I'm available as soon as I know. In fact I'm going to call my Solicitor now.

1. The attribution of film credits can be fraught with angst, mistrust and recrimination. Once-happy collaborators may become adversaries. In 2000 Hulse made a short film called *Hotel Central*. His long-time friend Joost van Veen (Dutch artist filmmaker) was a key collaborator – performing in the film, assisting on the shoot, helping develop ideas. Veen's credit for the film is *Guest* – for Hulse the highest possible acknowledgement (within the broader concept of *a hotel*) – but for the Dutch actor and filmmaker, it was perhaps not the most useful nor glamorous accolade. Hulse and van Veen remain firm friends, fondly

referring to one another in terms of Dutch hairstyles: *kaale* (baldy) van Veen and *beever* (mullet head) Hulse.

07.01.11 05:38h   Subject: Duthie Memorial Wood
                  From: Dan Brawley[1]

The trees[2] are doing nicely. The Atlantic white cedar – also known as the 'Scottish cedar' in this part of the world – is a resilient type – not afraid of drought or bouts of frigid air. I took the liberty of planting as many of the remaining trees as I could. There will soon be a Duthie forest.

1. Festival director, Cucalorus Film Festival (Wilmington, NC).
2. In 2010 Matt Hulse and Lucy Brown attended Cucalorus. Hulse suggested to Brawley that trees should be planted to help offset the carbon emissions of the transatlantic flights – not just for himself, but for all filmmakers attending the event.

13.01.11 08:43h   Subject: Pythons/Trains   From: Matt Hulse

Advance horrors: I am on another teetotal binge.[1] Am likely to bring this ghastly affliction with me to London. I won't let it spoil any fun.

1. Hulse manages addiction. He is publicly transparent about his experience, and encourages others to speak up.

13.01.11 08:43h   Subject: Re: Pythons/Trains   From: Nick Currey

You might have warned me you'd gone Methodist[1] *hides the 2093904905 year old single malt he bought for his friend and curses fate, missed conviviality and rues liver failure.*

1. Methodism, or the Methodist movement, is a group of historically related denominations of Protestant Christianity that derive inspiration from the life and teachings of John Wesley – of whom Nick Currey is a descendent.

31.01.11 15:41h   Subject: Re: Mr Palin (and incorporating) re: Socks
                  From: Matt Hulse

Did you say that Palin[1] lives round the corner from you? Do you have 'in' on him at all? I was talking to a publisher and they suggested – without any mention of my recent Pythonomania[2] – that he should write an intro to the book.

1. Michael Palin, English comedian, actor, writer, television presenter and one of the members of Monty Python. He later made a number of popular travel documentaries for television.

2. Lucy Brown astutely gifted Hulse a copy of *The Pythons: Autobiography by The Pythons* (Thomas Dunne Books, 2003). Hulse learned how the team's filmmaker Terry Gilliam devised animated interludes to create a flow from one disjointed, absurd sketch to another. Gilliam's work influenced director Hulse, editor Currey and animator Alan Brown as they developed the role of animation in *Dummy Jim*.

01.02.11 07:46h   Subject: Re: Re: Mr Palin (and incorporating) re: Socks   From: Nick Currey

Hampstead Heath. Not quite sure where. He writes letters in green ink to the local paper complaining about the public concerts at Kenwood House[3] makin' da noise an' havin' common-lookin' chemical khazis all over the place. I have no 'in' with him though. Other than that my dad is a strange amalgam of Palin and Cleese[4], in looks and mannerisms. I am of the faintly seedy opinion that about 60% of all British women have Palin as their fantasy dad/uncle/postman/lover/Father Christmas. He's the Python I always wanted to be, but fear in reality I'm probably Carol Cleveland[5] (without the breasts).

3. A former stately home also known as the Iveagh Bequest.
4. English actor, comedian, writer and film producer. One of the members of Monty Python.
5. British actress and comedian – the sole female performer in *Monty Python's Flying Circus*.

04.02.11 22:14h   Subject: DUMMY JIM   From: Matt Hulse

Could you provide me with a quote for the creation of a DUMMY JIM sign? Free standing and based upon the iconic Hollywood sign.

07.02.11 21:51h   Subject: Re: DUMMY JIM   From: Guy Bishop[1]

Bare minimum raw material cost is about £200 – making letters from 6mm MDF, with enough batons to make it stand up in an easel kind of way. A sheet of MDF is 8 foot by 4 foot. If the D is cut from a full sheet, then the wider letters (M's and the Y) would need to be made from a sheet and a bit in order to maintain the typeface proportions. You could squeeze them a little to save time and materials, or make the letters shorter. For easel-style, you're going to need a wind-free day.

1. Sculptor, mechanical model and prop maker. Created work for Hulse's short film *Half Life* (2004) and elaborate kinetic sculptures for *Harrachov* (2007).

sparkly-eyed, d-ream-y words. So the future is not so much bright as broken. Arse. We atheists are supposed to be cool with this, but I'm not; it pisses me off. But let's at least try to stare it out.

4. English physicist, and professor of particle physics in the School of Physics and Astronomy at the University of Manchester. Best known to the public as the presenter of science programmes.
5. BBC Radio 4 discussion programme (since April 1970).

15.03.11 09:26h   Subject: Re: Dummy Jim = Entropy
                   From: Matt Hulse

I am tipsy. Yes, time = death: that's what I was getting at. Jim Morrison[6] *will* have his day/point/residuals. Not sure I like the idea of a kind of 'zero degrees nebulous absence for eternity' situation but as the anaemic Auntie[7] explained, it's not for a while. Bowie[8] has a point. TIME TAKES A CIGARETTE. So. We film *you* drawing in 'real time' and as far as I can tell THAT'S A MOVIE. PS: If you ever feel down over the next days, just imagine this scene. I have sent the Rather Tight Pull-Over knitted by Jeni to Sam.[9] He has to try it on AND do exercises in it. In front of his betrothed, Mary[10], who you may recall is forceful.

6. American singer, songwriter and poet (1943–1971) best remembered as the lead singer of The Doors, sometimes referred to as "Lizard King" and "King of Orgasmic Rock". In 1947, the four-year-old Morrison witnessed a car accident in the desert, in which a family of Native Americans may have been killed. Morrison invokes this incident as a *momento mori* repeatedly in his songs and poems.
7. "A name first used in 1950s to contrast the BBC's prudish, cosy, puritanical 'refrained' image with that of the much brasher ITV." (BBC Written Archives)
8. English singer-songwriter, multi-instrumentalist, record producer, arranger, actor and secret admirer of Lucy Brown. "Time takes a cigarette / Puts it in your mouth" are the opening lines to *Rock 'n' Roll Suicide* (©1972 EMI Music Publishing, BMG Rights Management US, LLC, Tintoretto Music). These lyrics are similar to the poem *Chants Andalous* by Manuel Machado: *Life is a cigarette / Cinder, ash and fire / Some smoke it in a hurry / Others savour it.* (*The Complete David Bowie*, Nicholas Pegg, 2000). The transformation of tobacco to ash is a process of entropy sparked and accelerated by the smoker.
9. Jeni Reid knitted two sleeveless costume pullovers for the actor, one in royal blue, the other in a kind of dried out baked bean sauce hue, both based on a 1950s knitting pattern, *The Trimly Orthodox*. The dried out baked bean sauce version was originally conceived of as an *obligation knit* – perhaps a doting auntie had lovingly knitted it for Duthie and he felt obliged to take it on his

travels? The blue was conceived of as something he might be comfortable wearing out and about. In practice, the complex knitwear took longer than expected. In the film, the obligation knit became his go-to. The blue one is completed by Reid on camera, as part of the action.

10. Mary McFeeley.

15.03.11 09:49h   Subject: Re: Dummy Jim = Entropy
                  From: Nick Currey

Oh huzzah, you're tipsy, FINALLY. You had me worried. I've been editing on Leffe[11]. Great fun but not great for close edits. You get a bit Big Picture rather than God is in the Detail after a while. Mary – forceful? I'm trying to picture her. Wasn't there an accent? The thing I really remember was that her job involved standing up to criminally rude sheiks with erectile dysfunction.[12]

11. Premium Belgian beer brand owned by InBev Belgium, the European operating arm of the global Anheuser–Busch InBev brewery giant.

12. At that time, McFeeley was working at The Lister Fertility Clinic (London).

30.03.11 21:22h   Subject: Fishermen   From: Matt Hulse

The fishermen. In the journal these are named as Mr. Tait, Mr. Buchan and Mr. Third. On the morning of his departure, Jim shows them his pocket map of Europe and discusses his intended route to Morocco. Then off he pedals – it's a simple scene really, but a key one. In the film, we'll never know them by name – these are three guys that Jim sees pretty much everyday and is relaxed in the presence of – these characters represent *home*.

I'm not interested in going through casting sessions for these parts – the main thing is that the guys are willing to take part and are able to act 'natural'. Obviously I'll help them in this; we can rehearse with Sam, maybe ask them to learn some simple sign language for the different countries. The shoot will have an improvised approach and the scene a documentary feel.

31.03.11 04:10h   Subject: Re: Fishermen   From: Eunice Stephen

Mr. Tait. Mr. Buchan, and Mr. Third – could be anyone. Tait and Buchan are really popular surnames. To give you an example – I phoned someone the other day at a local engineering company – the receptionist asked *which Bruce Buchan?* – three Bruce Buchans from our village alone worked there. As you know we always refer to everybody by 'by-names'[1].

1. A non-hereditary name given to an individual in order to describe them in some way, for example *Convict Mackie*, *Fittie Bell*, *Stoops*, *Moleskin Jock*, *Mull's Mary*, *Tartan Annie*, *Jimmy Bargains*, *Coffee Jock*, *Scrow Dingwell* and *The Dummy* (or *Dummy Jim*).

09.04.11 05:16h   Subject: Re: GALLIVANT   From: Matt Hulse
Re. writing. Inside my heart – I think we should not enter into this pact. I value you so much as an older brother-in-disorderliness – but let's not go through the underwear draw, eh? I prefer that we drink beer together. Maybe shoot a film someday. Ben? He's very good at cards.

09.04.11 20:29h   Subject: Re: GALLIVANT   From: Andrew Kötting
a little relieved about the writing – started some notes which were a little fawning – so thank you for the let off. Eden calls – we must to more swimming

09.04.11 20:33h   Subject: Re: GALLIVANT   From: Matt Hulse
DAMN the academy. Go swimming.

13.04.11 19:23h   Subject: hi from the Broch[1]   From: Ainsley Dyga
Hi, just to let you know that Joy died yesterday. She had fallen and broken her hip at the weekend, she was taken in to surgery but didn't make it. Not sure if Lorraine would have had time to tell you.

13.04.11 19:55h   Subject: Re: hi from the Broch   From: Matt Hulse
Lorraine called me this morning and told me the sad news. Joy will be sorely missed. She was so welcoming, and very supportive as I began exploring ideas for the film. I have sent a card to Lorraine.

1. Fraserburgh. Scottish Gaelic: *A' Bhruaich*.

15.04.11 02:11h   Subject: Re: hi from the Broch   From: Ainsley Dyga
When you put the stone[2] up for Jim did someone tell you where to put it as Chrissie thinks it's on the wrong side?[3]

2. At the family's suggestion, the rights to Duthie's book *I Cycled Into The Arctic Circle* were assigned to film production company Tall Stories in return for

the creation of a headstone for the unmarked grave in which James and his mother Elizabeth are buried. At the time of writing, the rights to Duthie's book reside with Matt Hulse.

3. A centuries-old rivalry between the twin villages of Inverallochy and Cairnbulg – known collectively as Invercairn – persists to this day. There are no longer violent battles across the burn that once divided the two, and yet genuine loyalties remain. Those hailing from Cairnbulg are known as *Belgers* and those from Inverallochy as *Cottoners*.

15.04.11 02:56h Subject: Re: hi from the broch From: Matt Hulse

A&J Robertson (Granite) Aberdeen took charge of all the arrangements for the fixing of the stone. They checked the grave number with the local council. As it has been explained to me, Belgers are buried on the right hand side – as you walk in to the cemetery, with your back to the road – and Cottoners on the left. James lived on Main St, Cairnbulg: a Belger.

01.05.11 19:31h Subject: BSL[1] Lord's Prayer From: Samuel Dore

Hi Matt & Jo[2], I've been looking at BSL versions of The Lord's Prayer and came across these online videos. They got me thinking about how we will be portraying sign language in *Dummy Jim*. If we are making a film about a 1950s adventure I don't want to confuse audiences with contemporary BSL?

1. British Sign Language.
2. Jo Ross, BSL/English interpreter. Ross has supported Hulse, Dore and *Dummy Jim* for many years, interpreting not only in the literal sense of language translation, but also in the much trickier area of deaf community politics.

01.05.11 19:58h Subject: Re: BSL Lord's Prayer From: Matt Hulse

Don't worry about this. Most of the time you'll be too busy pedalling, erecting/dismantling a tent, gutting fish[3], learning how to resole a shoe[4], sewing patches on luggage, making shadows on the walls of your tent[5], eating baguette[6], etc.

3. This never happened.
4. Nor did this.
5. Nor this.
6. Dore ate an entire baguette.

01.05.11 20:41h Subject: Re: BSL Lord's Prayer From: Samuel Dore
This is becoming less of a film shoot and more of a Cubs'[7] adventure. I used to be a Cub and relished every moment of it.

7. The Cub scheme was started by The Boy Scouts Association in 1914, seven years after the foundation of the Boy Scouts, in order to cater to the many younger boys who were too young to be Boy Scouts but who wanted to be associated with Scouting.

01.05.11 20:52h Subject: Re: BSL Lord's Prayer From: Matt Hulse
PS: I was a cub too – hated it – so I shall be taking my fear, loathing and dampness out on you. Ok, maybe *hate* is a bit strong … but I have never liked things that felt 'organized', especially by middle-aged men in khaki pants. More to the point though, Croydon Cubs (imagine) was on Thursday evenings, and this clashed with *The Six Million Dollar Man*.[8]

8. American television series (1974–1978) about former astronaut Steve Austin, played by Lee Majors. This guy can run at speeds of 60mph. His eye has a 20:1 zoom lens and infrared capabilities, while his bionic limbs each have the power of a bulldozer.

01.05.2011 19:34h Subject: Follow The Master From: Samuel Dore
I forgot to mention that I have finally seen *Follow The Master*. It's a really nice film – even if I didn't know what the hell was going on. It's a lovely tribute to your family. Tippy was adorable as ever, a real star. I'm guessing this is the approach you'd like for Dummy Jim?

05.05.11 08:14h Subject: Up Here[1] From: Matt Hulse
Firstly may I say the folk here are lovely that it will be guaranteed a magical success even if you all die on stage. This is a tremendous part of the world, I am discovering. I suppose I shouldn't be too surprised, because Dummy Jim sprang out of here, but you know, it just *looks* so grey. We'll have Invercairn Community Hall for all of Friday. Lucy heard a rumour that the Line Dancing class will be 'taking a holiday'. So if you are happy to work around folk loading up tables with cakes and short bright-eyed assertive ladies speaking in sing-song[2] voices … you'll be fine.

Myself, Ian[3] and Gabz[4] will be mooching about with cameras too, trying to make sense of it. My mum is on the cooking so you'll be fed well.

1. Message sent from the *Dummy Jim* production base – two caravans in Strichen

– to members of The One Ensemble and Sarah Kenchington.
2. Local dialect *The Doric* is to this author's ear particularly melodic.
3. Ian Dodds. Director of Photography.
4. Gabriel Foster Prior. Production assistant, editor, filmmaker.

17.05.11 03:55h   Subject: Death Valley Radio Airplay Notice
                   From: Ron Alden
Thank you for providing a promotional copy of the *Dummy Jim* soundtrack album. I thought you'd like to know that Death Valley Radio[1] program 676 included the selections "Well-Painted Bicycle" and "Monique".

1. *"A carefully constructed, format-free program for the musically curious. Each week WNTI gives Ron the freedom to blend old, new, familiar and peculiar sounds, a mix that seems to work most of the time. New listeners are always welcome."* deathvalleyradio.org.

10.06.11 10:41h   Subject: A Wee Taster[1]   From: Matt Hulse
We'll know whether or not we need to shoot more with you by the end of June. What I am aiming for is a film with as little dialogue/explanation as possible – to tell it visually as far as I can – in which case we may not need you as 'narrator'. So it's less likely that you need to have that awful haircut again.

I must find the courage to leave the journal 'behind' and trust that the adaptation to screen has happened. In the end, a film can only offer a window on life. The 'making of' and 'preparation' threads running through the film will do the job of articulating Duthie's experience (albeit obliquely), so we won't need 'backing up' with explanation, or the reading out of lengthy sections of the journal.

I am happy for minimal sign language in the film after all. In the company of hearing folk, Duthie was a fingerspeller and note-writer, not a signer. To be true to this, we ought not really see Sam-as-Jim speedily signing away on screen, although I'm paranoid about being yet another hearing director who has stripped the BSL away, even though in the case of finger-speller-note-writer-Jim it's the logical thing to do.

1. Hulse sent a sample of roughly edited scenes from the shoot in Invercairn to folk closely involved with the project.

11.06.11 00:10h   Subject: Re: A Wee Taster   From: Samuel Dore
I have always had reservations about using British Sign Language in *Dummy Jim* – especially as the guy used fingerspelling or basic sign language. I also worry about audiences, particularly those who are well versed in sign language – people complaining the signing wasn't correct or whatever.

So I don't think you're doing anything wrong with taking the BSL out. This would help make the whole film feel more authentic, perhaps adding to the mythology of *Dummy Jim*. If Duthie connects too closely to audiences, this may weaken the impact of his character. In making him accessible to modern audiences, the fourth wall is broken – which might not work.

This is not a film exclusively for Deaf audiences; this is for everyone. The percentage of Deaf people watching this film will be very low compared to the percentage of hearing audiences.

Once again thanks very much for having faith in me, it's been a great experience and I enjoyed working with you and Ian so I'm very excited about the end result.

13.06.11 15:12h   Subject: Re: A Wee Taster   From: Matt Hulse
I am relieved that we see eye to eye. This area is fraught with politics and potential problems, but as we have discussed, the best way to break through is to make the best possible film, and then the 'issues' seem less important.

13.06.11 17:23h   Subject: Re: A Wee Taster   From: Svenja Würm[1]
I don't know what to say, this made me cry a little on this grey Monday morning. It's beautiful. Can't wait for the end product! Thanks.

1. Programme director of the European Master's in Sign Language Interpreting at Heriot-Watt University (Edinburgh). In 2006 Würm translated Hulse's screenplay for *Dummy Jim* into German. (See p.59).

17.06.11 22:19h   Subject: Multiverse   From: Matt Hulse
I have just completed a long letter to Michael Palin typed on a sheet of that lovely Panda Notepad you gave me last year. Attempting to get him creatively engaged with the book reprint aspect of the *Dummy Jim* multiverse.

18.06.11 00:10h   Subject: Re: Multiverse   From: Vicky Mohieddeen[1]
That fills me with joy :)

1. Curator, editor, filmmaker. Mohieddeen was briefly a student of Hulse's during his tenure as an ad-hoc tutor of Experimental Film at Edinburgh College of Art. After graduation she moved to Beijing (China) and established non-profit film screening organisation *Electric Shadows*.

18.06.11 10:07h   Subject: Re: Multiverse   From: Matt Hulse
Good. I am aware of the positivity you've been sending my way and this is a small action to recognize it and pass it on.

14.07.11 03:02h   Subject: Re: soul searchin'
                  From: Elizabeth Lawrence
If I had a dollar for every time somebody said to me "You still working on that cowboy movie?"[1] I'd be able to fund 10 new documentaries. Or the ever popular "You look tired, you should really take a step back... maybe take a vacation or something." I don't say to them: "You look tired, you should walk away from your three kids for a few months and get some rest!" We've chosen an epic film journey... and we have to remember that to *choose* is a beautiful thing. Not always the easiest thing to do, but the most rewarding.

1. Lawrence's documentary *Roll Out, Cowboy* tells the story of Chris "Sandman" Sand, a rapping cowboy from Dunn Center, North Dakota. Hulse saw the film at Cucalorus Film Festival (Wilmington NC) in 2010, the year of its release. Loving the film, and recognizing strong connections between mavericks Sandman and the inspiration for his own film – "*genuine gentlemen in stylish hats*" – he offered to help Lawrence bring the film to Scotland. The film toured nine venues in September 2011, along with a trailer for *Dummy Jim*.

19.07.11 07:37h   Subject: Re: cutler's fish   From: Nick Currey
I have been watching the footage shot by Duthie himself this evening.[1] It seems he didn't understand about focus – this footage has an other-worldly quality and an intensity of colour, like mini Gerhard Richter[2] paintings. He was keen to film himself – thus we have him parading about in Dutch clothing?

1. In May 2010, on the final day of the shoot, Duthie's own 16mm camera and reels of film were unearthed in an attic in St Combs (a few miles east of Invercairn). Vera Buchan and Alma Smith – who discovered the haul – agreed to the filmmakers' use of the material. They offered the camera to Hulse if the

film *Dummy Jim* "is any good." At the time of writing, the camera remains in St Combs.

2. German visual artist and one of the pioneers of the New European Painting that emerged in the second half of the twentieth century. His art follows the example of Picasso in undermining the concept of an artist's obligation to maintain a single cohesive style.

19.07.11 19:50h   Subject: Re: cutler's fish   From: Matt Hulse

True, and we can *work with* the lack of focus … imagine a bunch of soft images ensemble … a field of soft. That costume he's parading around in is from the very same shop that Tishna and I visited in Volendam, where we got dressed up and had our photo taken.[3]

3. In 2005 Hulse and Molla retraced Duthie's route through the UK, France, Belgium, Holland, Germany and Denmark, shooting Super 8mm. (See p.55).

12.07.12 13:01h   Subject: Regarding Dummy Jim   From: Matt Hulse

Hey Sam. Greetings from USA.[1] I was in Chicago last week and I thought about the fun we had at the Festival of Cinema for the Deaf.[2] I'm in the US until mid September 'trying out a new life' – with Elizabeth – also a filmmaker – imagine the amount of documenting going on. I feel happy, sad, excited, anxious, amazed, hot, unnerved, fine … all at once. In short, I am (still) alive.

Before I left the UK I took the opportunity to show Ian the completed rough edit. He made a suggestion that I found interesting and valuable.

We have used Duthie's original text verbatim from the journal as a form of captioning. These act like your/Jim's inner thoughts. Ian's point was that (for a hearing viewer) captions used in that way are usually accompanied by a voiceover – and that the absence of voice created a sense of distance from you as an actor/character. Would you agree to us recording your voice for narration?

1. Williamsburg, Brooklyn.
2. Founded in 2002 by Joshua Flanders, the first deaf film festival in North America. Inspired by the event, Hulse founded and programmed a similar event in the UK – *Sign Language Cinema* – that ran for three years (2002, 2003 and 2006) at Filmhouse (Edinburgh) and Glasgow Film Theatre.

12.07.12 16:49h   Subject: Re: Regarding Dummy Jim
              From: Samuel Dore

It makes sense – we need to reach out to as many audiences as possible.

However – I don't have the clearest voice. Hearing people might be thrown off by it? Picky film viewers might think there's something wrong with the audio – hearing audiences respond to the audio before the visuals. Then there's the matter of how my voice has a West Country twang![1] Happy to give it a try but maybe we should find out what Duthie's voice was really like?

1. Samuel Dore is from Bristol.

10.08.12 17:49h   Subject: Re: 'tats of Uzi's   From: Matt Hulse

I have been rubbish. Trash. All over the place emotionally and physically. I thought I might have had a better handle on 'shit' by now but just as I was, you know, sharpening my pencils for the new term[1] and setting out my drives neatly on a cheap, borrowed, wonky shelving unit, Elizabeth comes crashing down with post-NYC held-in grief, plus mounting tension as she awaits her final d.i.v.o.r.c.e papers. So imagine *Who's Afraid of Virginia Woolf*[2] colliding with *Nuts in May*[3] plus a bit of *Blue Velvet*[4] and you'll get a picture of all the fun of the fair.

1. Hulse and Lawrence moved to Wilmington (NC) to start their residency as artists at Cucalorus Film Festival.
2. 1962 play by Edward Albee. It examines the marriage breakdown of a middle-aged couple, Martha and George. The film adaptation (1966) was directed by Mike Nichols and stars Richard Burton and Elizabeth Taylor.
3. Teleplay devised and directed by Mike Leigh, originally broadcast as part of the BBC's *Play for Today* series (1976). A nature-loving and self-righteous couple battle to enjoy what they perceive to be the idyllic camping holiday.
4. Hair-raising 1986 American neo-noir mystery film written and directed by David Lynch, filmed on location in Wilmington (NC).

10.08.12 20:55h   Subject: Re: 'tats of Uzi's   From: Nick Currey

My God what's going on you lot? I thought you'd committed and all was marriage and Green Cards and tattoos of AK47s and pugs entwined?

The combination of *Who's Afraid*, *Nuts in May* and *Blue Velvet* makes me laugh out lewdly and yet wince in exquisite sympathy. Not a good mix – all are supremely histrionic, unsubtle and exhausting. In our dreams we inhabit a *Blue Velvet* world and maybe even like to think we are a character in the film. *Who's Afraid* is how we'd be if we were a bit cleverer. And yet the bleak aspects of co-existence take hold and cruelty becomes the rule, not the exception. Personally I'd always hope to have a scintilla of Burton in me. *Nuts in May* – almost certainly where we *actually* lurk – embarrassment, compromise, twee-ness, thwarted-ness, bluster and well-meaning, misguided perseverance.

23.09.12 02:53h   Subject: Re: Tiny Things Multiply
                   From: Nick Currey

I'm a bit drunk and just back from South London, but this sounds horrible! Maybe that's the point as it's about flies[1], but it sounds like an '80s synth nightmare, nothing like the Radiophonic[2] thing. Makes me think of bad pop played on the Simon Bates[3] show. I hate the '80s. Raymond Scott[4] may well have been the Gary Numan[5] of '59 but that's not something to be proud of. I'm waiting for the Swingle Singers[6], not Bros[7]. You hate me don't you? Well, I'm editing NHS bowel cancer statistics on my Sunday afternoon, so cut me some slack[8].

1. Jez Butler – composer of incidental music for *Dummy Jim* and partner to Polly Hulse (Matt's sister) – was commissioned to compose music for an animated interlude by Alan Brown that articulates Duthie's unfortunate encounter with *"Small, black insects … drinkers of human blood."* At the time of writing, Polly and Jez record and perform under the name *The Twelve Hour Foundation*, and the duo accompanied *Dummy Jim* on its tour of Scotland in July 2014.
2. BBC Radiophonic Workshop, created in 1958 to produce effects and new music for radio.
3. English disc jockey and radio presenter. Between 1976–1993 he worked at BBC Radio 1, presenting the station's weekday mid-morning show, with up to 11 million listeners.
4. American composer, band leader, pianist, engineer, recording studio maverick, and electronic instrument inventor.
5. English singer, songwriter, musician and record producer. Numan, whose signature sound consists of heavy synthesizer hooks fed through guitar effects pedals, is considered a pioneer of contemporary electronic music.
6. Vocal group, formed in 1962 in Paris (France) by Ward Swingle with Anne Germain, Jeanette Baucomont, Jean Cussac, Christiane Legrand and others.
7. British band active in the late 1980s and early 1990s, consisting of twin brothers Matt Goss and Luke Goss, with Craig Logan.
8. When not collaborating/arguing with Hulse, Currey edits educational and corporate videos.

02.12.12 01:43h   Subject: Sound Design   From: Matt Hulse

I have been sitting here alone in North Carolina[1] trying to find the best creative framework for the sound design. What I am after is rhythm, impacts, washes of enveloping sound, punctuations, sub-bass booms.

265

And then I thought: drum kit/percussion. Record one set up properly and create a rich palette of choice sounds and options, then take these into the digital domain to give them space and texture.

1. Following a disastrous, emotionally-fraught and mutually-destructive few months with Hulse in Wilmington, Lawrence returned briefly to New York, and then sought the security/comfort of her ex-husband and dogs in Los Angeles. Hulse persisted in Wilmington until Christmas, despite being officially ejected from his residency by the board of Cucalorus. He slept on the floor of a temporary studio using prop blankets from *Dummy Jim* as bedding. He showered and shaved at the Wilmington Family YMCA. During this period he completed his application for an EB1 Green Card, eventually leading to his recognition by the US immigration authorities as *An Alien of Extraordinary Ability* (as of 6th June 2013). Hulse composed this message two months into a period of sobriety that lasted until mid August 2013.

09.12.12 23:25h   Subject: dummy jim   From: Anna Abrahams[1]
Just watched Dummy Jim. I'm happy that you managed to find such a fitting form to tell your story. Your actor is lovely, the music wonderful, and the knitting masterful. I could go on about the rain, the dreams, the bike – it all falls into place.

One little thing. Before the film begins you have a citation from the book. Jim writes about the truth and faith he found in his travels. Are you not afraid to lose audience who will think it to be a 'Jesus-film'? Once you get to love Jim, know his background, the time and place he lived in, you accept that of course Christianity is part of his culture. But if you start so early in the film with 'faith', it could work against him. If I were you, I would just skip this last part of the sentence.

Another strange thing is that Jim says in the end that he 'heard many strange conversations'. Is 'heard' really his text?

1. Dutch filmmaker, author and film curator. Project leader and programmer for EYE Film Institute (Netherlands). Hulse provided the narration for her trilogy of short films *5 Walks. Hercynia Silver* (2008), *Desert 79°: 3 Journeys Beyond the Known World* (2010) and *7 Peaks* (2012).

17.12.12 08:51h   Subject: Re: dummy jim   From: Matt Hulse
We listened to what you said, and we have altered the text at the beginning. It's a tricky to get this guy's faith across accurately without people thinking that I – personally – am evangelizing.

The second point – about 'heard' – yes, it's his actual text – in general we have altered his words hardly at all. The above is an exception. Deaf people often talk of hearing/listening. Hearing is done in the brain, not really in the ear. The ear is just a funnel for sound. Don't think about that too much or you will realize that your brain is rather exposed to the elements.

21.12.12 02:40h   Subject: Ch-Ch-Ch-Ch-Changes   From: Matt Hulse
Word spreads fast in Mid-Winter so you may have already heard, but I have decided (after a LOT of brain, heart, lung, organ and soul searching) *not* to hold the UK premiere of Dummy Jim at GFF[1]. It's a long story, but the nutshell I can offer is: on behalf of all the people who have been involved in the project for years, I need to place the film in the very strongest possible position for UK theatrical release and attention, and the feedback I could glean universally erred on the side of EIFF[2].

1. Hulse originally negotiated to hold the UK premiere of *Dummy Jim* at the Glasgow Film Festival.
2. Edinburgh International Film Festival, where *Dummy Jim* held its UK premiere on 20th June 2013.

21.12.12 04:31h   Subject: Re: Ch-Ch-Ch-Ch-Changes
             From: Matt Lloyd[2]
Yes, no, that's understandable, though there are a lot of disappointed people here, so if you'll permit me to be fatherly for a second and wag my finger, maybe you should have thought about that before you approached GFF.

2. Director of the Glasgow Short Film Festival, friend and one of the Kindly Folk.

21.12.12 04:48h   Subject: Re: Ch-Ch-Ch-Ch-Changes
             From: Matt Hulse
That's awful to hear. There's nothing I find more upsetting than disappointing people. *Dummy Jim* is a poem about my dedication to people. It's not some flippant choice I've made; I've been completely torn. I don't suppose I can expect anyone to understand for some time to come, but in the end I have had to make a decision that is best *for the film* and those involved – not for *me* – based upon the available facts and advice. One day perhaps I will get a chance to explain what this past year has been like – frankly, I'm glad that I am still sane. It's amazing that I even finished the damned film.

267

14.01.13 03:20h   Subject: I'm the knitter not the sound guy
From: Jeni Reid

Are these meows[1] any good? The background noise is me trying to open a tin of tuna. I nearly lost a leg when he got fed up of playing and rugby tackled me in the living room. Will Magnus become an overnight sensation? He's hard enough to live with without an ego the size of a horse. I'll keep his expectations low by feeding him budget cat food. Loving my membership of the *Dummy Jim* team – more grateful than Magnus who is sitting in a corner licking his arse.

1. At a very late stage in the edit of *Dummy Jim*, Reid was asked to provide recordings of her cat.

17.01.13 18:03h   Subject: Update   From: Jez Butler

Had a second night of mixing *Roondaboot*[1] dreams. Night before last involved me holding a microphone to the speakers to capture part of it for the film – me thinking 'this'll sound crap'. Last night was all to do with the synth fade-in.

1. Song composed by Matt Hulse for the closing credits of *Dummy Jim* performed by Ludwig (Matt Hulse, Polly Hulse, Jez Butler and Elizabeth Lawrence).

05.02.13 00:57h   Subject: Tigerzzz   From: Ian Francis[1]

Condolences on the lack of Tiger[2] action.

1. Director of Flatpack Film Festival, co-founded with Pip McKnight in Birmingham (UK) 2006.
2. *Dummy Jim* was one of 15 films nominated for a *Hivos Tiger Award* at International Film Festival Rotterdam 2013. The production awards – worth €15,000 each – are granted by an international jury to the filmmakers of the three best films from the competition.

05.02.13 01:17h   Subject: Re: Tigerzzz   From: Matt Hulse

You catch me fresh from photographing dirty net curtains in suburban Rotterdam windows. Usual story. The Tiger thing was weird. I'm sure I don't need to tell you that 'classic European issue-based long-take drama' won the day – with a nod to the developing world of course. My films are Too Hearty and Too Much Fun for this cut'n'thrust. But then again I did set out to make *Bedknobs and Broomsticks*[3] so you get what you deserve. I was rather thrilled when at the final Q&A *Dummy Jim* was described as 'a kind of musical'. Perhaps that's next?

3. A 1971 American musical film produced by Walt Disney Productions based upon the books *The Magic Bed Knob; or, How to Become a Witch in Ten Easy Lessons* (1943) and *Bonfires and Broomsticks* (1945) by English children's author Mary Norton. The film, which combines live action and animation, stars Angela Lansbury and David Tomlinson.

11.02.13 19:13h   Subject: hi   From: Tricia Hulse[1]

Sorry about the Tiger – that's life. I assume you are in chilly Scotland somewhere. It's cold and trying to snow here so I guess you are colder.

1. Step-mother to the Hulse children since c.1979.

14.02.13 01:54h   Subject: Re: hi   From: Matt Hulse

I can tell you that I knew within watching the first three clips of the other nominated films that it was not to be *Dummy Jim's* night. So I immediately relaxed and absorbed the bizarre horse-trading, sipped wryly at my non-alcoholic drink, and was gratified by the fact that I had second-guessed the jury. What else? I have learned that not only did Joe Strummer[2] share my 21st August birth date, he also retreated to the art room to escape games, smoked dried banana skins, dreamed of being a cartoonist, had a lot of nervous energy and stamina, was a middle child and recognized music as a door to freedom.

2. British musician, singer, actor and songwriter. Co-founder, lyricist, rhythm guitarist and lead vocalist of The Clash, a punk rock band formed in 1976.

19.04.13 06:19h   Subject: Re: the quiet life   From: Tadhg O'Sullivan[1]

I love Dummy Jim. It's a bold celebration of boldness itself: the boldness of a man embarking on a willfully odd and joyful undertaking being met (60-odd years later) by a man willing to put the joy central to that adventure foremost in a film that bears not a hint of irony nor self-regard.

1. Filmmaker, editor, wanderer, failed inventor.

23.05.13 14:22h   Subject: Re: Interview Questions   From: Matt Hulse

HJ:[1] *The structure of the film moves between the re-enactment of James's journey, and the community living in Invercairn, and their memory of him. Why did you choose to form the narrative this way?*

A key aspect of my work in moving image over the past 20+ years has been an exploration of the structures, patterns and the processes of filmmaking. I am more influenced by the structures found in poetry, music or print design than by screenplays or other films. Someone cleverer than I once said that it was the filmmaker's job *to put two and two together but let the audience make four*. My motivation is to gently reveal and share these structures with the viewer, to encourage them into a new way of watching a film, rewarding them for putting in the work of deciphering the film's internal logic. I hope this is empowering for the viewer.

I'm not interested in giving genre or technique priority over form. If the best way to articulate the sequences in Duthie's book is with a combination of animation and documentary, then (budget permitting) let's try and make that work.

When I approached the adaptation I was looking at it from the perspective of an artist, asking: what's the intrinsic truth I see buried here and how can I reveal that using juxtapositions of recorded image and sound? Can I get the feel of the-book-in-the-hand up there on the screen?

It's complicated to explain in words, that's maybe why I make films. But that's partly how the 'narrative' ended up being set out in this way. It's more like a musical score – several interwoven threads that evolve and resolve over the course of 87 minutes. It's also a film about the inevitability of death, and that life goes on, and that everything is a cycle. The oldest story we know, but as told through knitwear, baking, masonry, cycling and landscape.

HJ: *The folkloric aspects of Dummy Jim reminded me of Andrew Kötting's work, and also Jeremy Deller[2] with this focus on community collaboration. What were your reference points for making the film?*

Kötting and Deller are a few years older than me but essentially I fall under the same set of influences as them. That's where the connections are. Art school, punk, performance/intervention art, DIY mavericks, embracing happenstance, community/family engagement. It's about fostering and harnessing a kind of benign creative chaos. I'm happy for you to set my name alongside them. I consider them artists who place integrity high on their list, and who work with the power of absurdity. I don't know if it's folkloric, but it's an approach that likes folk.

1. Helen Jack, film curator and creative producer, documentary editor for UK-based filmmakers network, Shooting People.
2. British conceptual, video and installation artist. Much of Deller's work is collaborative. It has a strong political aspect, in the subjects dealt with and also

the devaluation of artistic ego through the involvement of other people in the creative process.

29.05.13 17:16h   Subject: Jim Lad   From: Archie Ramsay[1]
Matt ya bugger! Many, many congratulations on the Invercairn[2] screening! You sure done good, ma boy! I took the liberty of feeling very proud of you in Rotterdam[3], and I'm taking the liberty of being super-proud of you now.

1. Jeni Reid's husband.
2. Private community screening of *Dummy Jim* at Invercairn Community Hall on 29th June 2013.
3. *Dummy Jim* world premiere at International Film Festival Rotterdam 28th January 2013.

29.05.13 17:53h   Subject: Re: Jim Lad   From: Matt Hulse
I am proud of nothing; all will falter in a bitter wind-blasted plume of ash, chased by the incoming rain, and nothing nice for tea. Calvin.[4]

4. French theologian and pastor during the Protestant Reformation. Principal figure in the development of the system of Christian theology later called Calvinism, aspects of which include the doctrine of predestination and the absolute sovereignty of God in salvation of the human soul from death and eternal damnation.

29.05.13 18:07h   Subject: Re: Jim Lad   From: Archie Ramsay
That's OK then.

18.07.13 01:14h   Subject: hi   From: Eunice Stephen
Have spent the whole day gardening and am now going to tackle the ironing after a cup of tea. I still have a really good memory of the screening. My dad[1] regrets he didn't give you a standing ovation; but that is not really Invercairn style.

1. Robert 'Bobby' Stephen features in *Dummy Jim* as the lay preacher (see pp.112–113). He offered Hulse a wealth of advice upon local religious and esoteric matters, mostly via fascinating and densely composed hand-written letters.

18.07.13 01:29h   Subject: Re: hi   From: Matt Hulse
That's a very sweet comment from Bobby. I would have been aghast at a standing ovation – that only really happens in films, or dreams,

I think? The audience? Respectful, kind and engaged – I shall never forget it. One of my great grandmothers hailed from Macduff so I understand reserve.[2]

2. Mary Simpson. Macduff is 28.3 miles west of Inverallochy.

20.07.13 23:24h   Subject: Re: Tea?   From: Matt Hulse

Hey VMO[1]. Sorry to have missed you as you passed through London. My life has gotten a bit f*cked up and I am not the greatest company. I hear you re. China. Please don't think that I am not interested. Safe travels.

1. Vicky Mohieddeen. The China-based *Electric Shadows* curator had screened a number of Hulse's short films, including the *Dummy Jim* teaser *God Gives Nuts But He Does Not Crack Them* (2006), which she presented to a class of Beijing school children. The pair were involved in ongoing discussions regarding a possible screening of Hulse's debut feature *Follow The Master* on the Great Wall of China.

07.09.13 18:04h   Subject: Re: Knitted Food   From: Jeni Reid

Today's job will be searching for knitted egg patterns.[1] I have one for a knitted eyeball so that is a start. Scotch eggs[2] are rounder than real eggs aren't they?

1. Reid led a community food-knitting workshop at the *Berwick Film & Media Arts Festival* (2013) culminating in a woolen picnic of knitted lollipops, sandwiches and cakes for the *Dummy Jim* installation *Better To Wear Out Shoes Than Sheets*, commissioned by the festival.
2. Scotch eggs re-appear as a motif in Hulse's short film *Within The Firmament Of The Edible* (2014), commissioned by The Andrew Raven Trust.

07.09.13 16:51h   Subject: Guardian Travel Article   From: Nick Currey

Do you know why the rather banal story of you receiving the book from your mother[1] is the one thing that the press always mentioned?

1. Ruth Pendragon unearthed a hardback copy of Duthie's *I Cycled Into The Arctic Circle* (1955) when she was working at Angus Johnston's *Iona Bookshop* in 2000. She sent this to her son Matt with a note that read: *PS: don't feel you have to turn the enclosed into a film …*

07.09.13 22:38h   Subject: Re: Guardian Travel Article
                  From: Matt Hulse

People love a good story and a bit of 'romance' (in its broadest sense), right? *'Mother discovers unknown gem on remote island and inspires son to Great Art'*. It's the human angle. An angle we might need, given that most of the film is just shots of Sam staring at food or luggage.

14.09.13 23:42h   Subject: Mamo Mozel   From: Matt Hulse

Just going through some kids' artwork.[1] Here's an impression of Jim's time in France. Accurate? (See p.31).

1. As part of the Hulse's planned cultural engagement activities around the making of *Dummy Jim*, Edinburgh bookbinder and paper artist Rachel Hazzell was commissioned to lead book-making workshops at Inverallochy School.

14.09.13 23:42h   Subject: Re: Mamo Mozel   From: Nick Currey

Ah yes, the famous passage about having energetic sexual congress with blonde ladies whilst smoking with a cigarette holder and wearing a golden crown. I think he's ordering German wine too, just to rub it in.

06.10.13 02:11h   Subject: Ukulele?   From: Matt Hulse

It has become something of a tradition for me to intro the film with a song by Ivor Cutler[1] on the ukulele. Do you know anyone who has one I might borrow for the screening?[2] The song is used to get the audience involved[3] – in humming. The same humming that is used on the soundtrack to vibrate theatre walls: a physically 'felt' sound. Perhaps our deaf audience might drum their feet if not humming?

1. Scottish poet, songwriter and humorist. Screenings of *Dummy Jim* are often been preceded by a live performance of Cutler's song *Beautiful Cosmos*. The song first appeared on Cutler's album *Jammy Smears* (1976). It also appears in Hulse's adaptation of T. S. Eliot's *The Love Song of J. Alfred Prufrock* (1989), an epic Super 8mm film co-directed by his brother Toby Hulse.
2. Opening night of the film's six-week theatrical release at EYE Film Institute (Amsterdam).
3. Hulse invites the audience to hum an unbroken, single note in unison – a drone – similar to that created by Cutler's harmonium, or a bagpipe, or the *om shanti* mantra.

07.10.13 00:40h   Subject: Re. Ukulele?   From: Anna Abrahams

You know you are insane, and that is exactly why I am so fond of you.

06.07.14 Audience Feedback from the GFT after the Opening Night of
Dummy Jim: A Wee Tour[1]
What three words would you use to describe your experience of the event?

Beautiful, surprising, moving.
Atmospheric, cultural, eccentric.
Eye opening, intelligent, thoughtful.
Uplifting, fulfilling, satisfying.
Impressed, challenged, involved.
Visionary, fascinating, engaging.
Stressful – ultimately uplifting.

Any comments you would like to make?

Intriguing, moving narrative threads spun from apparently nothing.
Great cinema. An inspiring story told in a fresh, exciting way.
Love seeing films with the director there. Good band.
I'd suggest giving people the option to leave.

1. In July 2014, accompanied by electronica duo *The Twelve Hour Foundation*, Hulse organized an eleven date Scottish tour of *Dummy Jim*, calling in on Glasgow, Glenesk, Wick, Huntly, Banchory, Mintlaw, Inverness, Portsoy, Strathdon, Edinburgh and North Berwick.

07.07.14 21:57h   Subject: Glasgow Launch   From: Stevie Jones[1]
Thanks so much for the comps last night. The film is utterly inspiring. I was moved beyond belief and blown away by its inventiveness and unique perspective. Thought the music worked wonderfully with picture to create a sum greater than parts – enjoyed the tight editing to sound. The triumphant homecoming scene was totally jaw dropping! The film has the depth of a project that has taken a long time to complete. Every year's paid off – like a vintage wine.

1. Sound engineer who recorded and mixed the *Dummy Jim* soundtrack album.

18.10.14 03:25h   Subject: Magnus   From: Jeni Reid
I think Magnus would have loved Jim to post a message about his passing. He was a diva; it makes me happy to think that he will now move on into the realm of legend. He'd already had an X-ray which showed no sign of a tumour but that was some months ago. Whatever he had was fast growing. He was slowing down and not enjoying his

food – for a greedy cat, a very bad sign indeed. It was kinder to let him go when he was already sedated. You'll be glad to know that he bit me as I put him into the cat basket for the last time.

09.04.15 15:00h   Subject: Dummy Jim Goodies
                   From: John Cunningham

I just returned from 3 weeks work offshore. Got my goodies.[1] I felt like Tommy Cooper[2] – every time I put my hand in the wee bag I'd pull out something else.

I love movies. I tend to let them wash over me. I try not to analyze them along the way. I deliberately didn't research anything about Duthie, so had no idea how the film would go. After a hard day at the nursing home, my wife Linda had fallen asleep beside me on the settee. As the choir sang and the final scene unfolded, I sobbed quietly so as not to wake her. A wee gem – one of those I'll watch again.

1. Cunningham purchased a Special Edition DVD and a limited edition artist's book from *Dummy Jim*'s online shop. Each of the 104 Bolton Twill cloth wallets contains hand-made, unbound inserts created by Alice Smith, Bracketpress and Matt Hulse for the *Edinburgh International Book Festival* event *Unbound* (2010).
2. Welsh prop comedian and magician (1921–1984).

21.05.15 16:33h   Subject: Re: Good To My Word   From: Sera Irvine[1]

Love the conversations; you couldn't make it up.[2]

1. Artist, curator and minder of dog Kep.
2. Hulse forwarded an example of his work-in-progress on this book.

22.05.15 03:01h   Subject: Re: Good To My Word   From: Matt Hulse

Yes, impossible to invent; that's what's so great. I was worrying about *writing a book* when in fact it had happened already, because I am constantly writing and broadcasting. In the past, folk would publish their learned journals towards the end of their lives – as advised by their agents – to maximize income. Literature in the early 20th century – pre digital multimedia – was desperate to leap off the page. My own private *Ulysses*[3] haunts me – or could that be my Grandpa Steve Jump.[4]

3. Novel by Irish writer James Joyce considered one of the most important works of modernist literature. According to Declan Kiberd: *Before Joyce, no writer of fiction had so foregrounded the process of thinking.* Proponents of

Ulysses such as Anthony Burgess have described the book as inimitable, and also possibly mad.

4. John Davies Jump, son of a baker, was the first in his family to get a place at university, in this case the University of Liverpool. On graduation he taught at a school in Holywell, North Wales, then during the Second World War he served in North Africa as the Captain of an artillery unit. On returning to civilian life he secured employment at Manchester University, where he remained for his academic career, progressing from junior to senior lecturer, then to Reader in English Literature. From 1966–76 he was the John Edward Taylor Professor of English Literature and concurrently the pro-Vice Chancellor of Manchester University. He wrote and/or edited several scholarly works, most notably on Byron, Tennyson, Dickens and Elizabethan drama. His daughter Ruth adds: *Everyone remembers him for his warmth, genuineness, integrity and passion for education. Very funny. Very modest.*

27.05.15 20:53h   Subject: image batch schedule
From: Christian Brett[1]

If any of the people you're commissioning essays from are academics, then you need to impress on them a given deadline. Academics have no real notion of what a deadline is. By their very nature they can never, ever quite finish anything to their own satisfaction and will forever make minor changes for as long as they are invited or allowed to. (And you can quote me on that.)

1. Typesetter of this book, Bracketpress, Rochdale.

27.05.15 23:16h   Subject: Fate   From: Robert Trueman

The worldly traveller ending his days alone on a quiet British road is an enigma no less mysterious than the fate of T. E Lawrence.[1]

1. Thomas Edward Lawrence. British archaeologist, military officer, and diplomat. Internationally famous as *Lawrence of Arabia* – the title used for the 1962 film based on his First World War activities, including the Sinai and Palestine Campaign, and the Arab Revolt against Ottoman Turkish rule of 1916–18. In 1935, Lawrence was fatally injured in a motorcycle accident in Dorset, when he swerved to avoid cyclists – thus, figuratively speaking, *Taking the Wall*, as Ixion advised (see email from Nick Currey dated 01.01.10).

28.05.15 02:16h   Subject: Re: Fate   From: Matt Hulse

Well Bertie[2] that ensures your inclusion in the book.

2. Hulse's nickname for his friend – of uncertain origin.

21.06.15 00:12h   Subject: POT THROWING   From: Matt Hulse

A dream I had. I was in a café at a film festival somewhere sat opposite a journalist – some 'cool' bloke with a lanyard. He said "Sorry to hear about *The Jarman Award*."[1] My face must have dropped a bit – at this point I still don't know the outcome.[2] He said, "Oh, sorry, you didn't hear yet? Anyway, *Dummy Jim* sounds really interesting, I'd like to see it. I hear there's a great pot-throwing scene?"

Then I woke up and strangled the cat.[3]

1. *"Celebrating the spirit of experimentation, imagination and innovation in the work of UK artist filmmakers, the Jarman Award recognizes individual artist filmmakers whose risk-taking work resists boundaries and conventional defini-tion – work that encompasses innovation, excellence and vision. The award shines light on artist filmmakers who are to our times what Jarman was to his."* (filmlondon.org.uk). Derek Jarman was an English film director, stage designer, diarist, artist, gardener and author. In 1991 Hulse wrote to Jarman, inviting him to his final year show of films at the University of Reading. Jarman's hand-written reply – in purple ink – explains graciously how he was unable to attend due to his film *The Garden* being screened at the Moscow International Film Festival. In 1979, the 11 year old Hulse was taken by his mother to see Jarman's adaptation of *The Tempest* at the Cambridge Arts Theatre.
2. For a second time, Hulse was nominated but not short-listed for the award.
3. Vicky Mohieddeen's cat George.

21.06.15 16:05h   Subject: Re: POT THROWING   From: Nick Currey

Shame we had to lose the pot-throwing scene. It was good but didn't add to the story arc. Is 'strangling the cat' a euphemism for something? I'm in a Sidmouth[4] bed pretending to be asleep while my grumpy girl-friend has a shower next door. A whippet[5] snoozes beside my battered liver. Cheers.

4. Town situated on the English Channel coast in Devon, South West England.
5. Harry.

04.06.15 00:38am   Subject: Reviews   From: Eunice Stephen

Today the whole school watched *Dummy Jim*. We munched popcorn and at half time scoffed Peter's ice cream[1]. Afterwards we wrote reviews for your book.

1. Peter's Ices is an award-winning ice cream manufacturer in Cairnbulg, run by owners Elizabeth and Peter McLennan.

277

24.06.15 02:50h   Subject: 4th Revised Proof   From: Matt Hulse
Fantastic work. Exciting to see it all come together. I'd like to show the raggedy edges and the kind of mess that only kids can make; the integrity of the way they fold things and colour outside the boundaries. Not sure we need boobs – nor Grandpa? The Tay Bridge Disaster seems a nice way to round things off. (See pp.214–215).

07.07.15 17:13h   Subject: Re: 4th Revised Proof   From: Alice Smith
I've been ill these last few days – hot water bottles in July! Hold fire on editing the email correspondence. I want to consider using an alternative cheaper printer. We sent a much smaller book to print with them. As soon as a copy returns, we'll make a judgment. If all's well and of high enough standard then we might be able to reconfigure specifications, and up the page extent to a maximum of 300pgs – but only if the print and binding is good enough.

08.07.15 13:19h   Subject: Re: 4th Revised Proof   From: Matt Hulse
I hope you are eating fruit. Although if you're anything like Uncle Smiffy[1] then you'll consider fruit *something that's there to look pretty.*

Thanks too for the advice – I'll hold back the biggest cleaver then. What I have so far reads well – in terms of working as a story in its own right about the project, about my relationships with people, about the process of art – and failure.

I hope you will consider doing the COVER. For my author portrait, I am working with Vicky on a pastiche of photographic portraits[2] of Beckett[3], Jean Luc Godard[4] and Eisenstein[5].

1. Mark Smith.
2. Hulse noticed striking similarities between portraits – shot years apart – of the directors mentioned. Each is holding a strip of celluloid film up to a source of light, as if examining the frames. Beckett and Godard are also smoking.
3. Samuel Beckett. Irish avant-garde novelist, playwright, theatre director and poet. His work offers a bleak, tragicomic outlook on human nature, coupled with black comedy and gallows humour.
4. At the Split International Festival of New Film (Croatia, 2001) Hulse's short film *Hotel Central* was jointly awarded the *Special Award for Film*, along with Jean Luc Godard for his feature length film *Eloge de l'Amour*.
5. Soviet Russian film director and film theorist; pioneer in the theory and practice of montage.

278

I CYCLED INTO THE ARCTIC CIRCLE

14.07.15 Beijing 22:37h   Handwritten letter From Matt Hulse
to his mother Ruth Pendragon

Dear Mum

I cycled to a café bar called *Beetle In A Box: Former Waiting For Godot*. Seriously, that's its name. Chinese English is literal, verbose and slightly incorrect all at once – perhaps the best kind of English. It is 39°C – couldn't be less like Jim's Arctic. I have just ordered a *Long Island Iced Tea*[1], a drink of extraordinarily good value and fortitude.

I'm in the final throes of the *Dummy Jim* project, one that has culminated in the book you hold in your hands. It was Vicky's suggestion that you would receive this letter only once the book was in print. I'm aware of a desire to resolve the project in a shapely, trimly and well-considered manner, to assert an impression of control over what has been a sprawling, sometimes haphazard process, one that has helped propel me to this point in time and space.

I have been looking for devices to help me bow out cyclically – *Dummy Jim* being about bicycles, circles, holes in shoes, tyres and ice, loops, return journeys, roundabouts, resurrection and so on. Having started with a book you sent me, it seems fitting to resolve these matters 15 years later with another book. Give me a book; I'll write you one back. That would make a neat and trimly finish – a closed circuit – but I'm afraid to say that it's *not yet quite over*.

As you know, I have endured multiple relocations these few years past – some chosen, others forced – and lest we forget those months of breakdown in *Alain's Room*[2]. Anyway, during the move to our new place, Graham Greene's[3] novel *The End of the Affair*[4] bobbed to the surface of a pile of *intransigent things*[5]. I picked it out; I do generally favour a slim pocket volume with a sober-looking and well-designed cover.[6]

Not being happy with yet more upheaval – despite moving to an adorable *ping fang*[7] at the very heart of Beijing, with a view of a pumpkin patch, protected from the craziness of 21,150,000+ busy people by palatial red wooden doors – Greene's book perhaps offered an immediate escape from and buffer against the chaos of dislocation.

Toby on family holidays comes to mind, his nose pressed into the comforting cleavage of a beloved book: *Swallows and Amazons*[8] and the distractions of Titty, obstinately refusing to acknowledge the present.

On the matter of siblings, allow me to put this down on paper. As they grow, brothers and sisters must divide up whatever spoils and powers life affords them. These 'choices' soon define the child and it's difficult to redefine oneself in the eyes of the family at a later date. I was never recognized as the sibling who was 'good with words' – partly because my schooling excluded Latin as a subject. This has always rankled somewhat. I placed top or second in the Spelling Bee for months on end and also sailed through English, both literature and language.

A dictionary-wielding family obsessed with typographical error and the 'correct' use of language can be a frustrating environment for the creative writer in their midst. Having said that, it is I who am now the published author, so was it perhaps the perfect literary hothouse?

Incidentally, I could also smash a ball way out of the court during a game of rounders. Despite repeating this game-winner several times during a particularly hot summer, the feat failed to win the heart of the ever-so-ordinary-but-I-loved-her-probably-because-she-was-a-blonde, Stephanie Caston. If you are reading this, Stephanie – Dollar's *Shooting Star*[9] was a piece of crap – and Simon Dunk? He was a *fake* punk.

Writing a book – as it turns out – is much harder than hitting a home run.

Is it perfume from the fur hood of a snorkel parka that makes me so digress? I grow cold; I grow old. I shall tear my bottom on the Bracket-press.[10]

Where were we? I'm writing to you about this book of Greene's. In a stream of published communications, this letter is my final strike; may this be the home run.

Sometimes one's life intersects with a work of art and the timing is perfect. Greene is keenly – devastatingly – astute on matters of the heart. His book, in rising to the surface of stuff, found a seriously disillusioned artist film maker, just shy of his 47th birthday, looking to understand why he should bother anymore – with art, love, life.

He opens the book with these words:

"A story has no beginning or end: arbitrarily one chooses that moment of experience from which to look back or from which to look ahead."

I don't torture myself with the hope that any day soon – if ever – I will comprehend what caused my 12+ year relationship with Lucy to fall apart, and so horribly. We betrayed one another in ugly, hurtful ways; *we were better than that*. I am ashamed of what unfolded, and yet we were both seemingly powerless at the time to have it unfold in any other way.

Did my determination to complete *Dummy Jim* help destroy our relationship? Possibly. Partly. And yet it also provided us with focus, definition, and – at times – joy. Sadly – over several years – trust, faith and patience somehow drained away: the principles of a healthy intimate human relationship seemed lost to us.

Greene understood this (inevitable?) decline, and he articulates it with startling clarity, wryness and bitter wit. Sometimes it's a genuine comfort to bask in the keenly observed and well-articulated chagrin of others.

Art: the original co-counsellor.

He also knew the sheer horror and destruction that can be aroused by intense sexual passion, such as I experienced fitfully for at least two years with Elizabeth. That devilish green-eyed sickness stifles the mind and gnaws away at our sense of security. From below the belt, the sex organs roar, destabilizing the mind's authority; the heart is pummeled like a cheap bolster caught between two selfish squabbling siblings: Duty and Abandon.

Like author Bendrix, I found myself creatively incapacitated for months on end, unable to focus on completing the film. Without Nick's love, resolve and inner Methodism the film would never have reached the screen.

Better To Wear Out Shoes Than Sheets opines *Dummy Jim* from beyond the grave, without a hint of irony: words that I chose to put amongst his signing hands. Is *Dummy Jim* perhaps little more than a complicated and extended *note to self*? It's certainly useless as a cycling manual and teaches us little of 'real' history.

In Greene's time, the telephone offered lovers fragmented, broken lines of communication. In mine, texts and video calls create an even more tempting illusion of contact. Cruelly divided by differences of time, an uncaring Atlantic ocean and, worse, a common language[11] – the centre could not hold, and things just fell apart.[12]

What does any of this have to do with Dummy Jim? Behold! A chorus of pedants, hands raised, enquiring in that tone of condescension that certain audience members adopt. Having watched an epic 87 minute long film that took many people 12 years to complete, they come away with little else than a fault: *fields of oilseed rape did not exist in 1951.* Why do people *do* that?

O! Hear Me, Pickers of Nits! It's all about the transformative power of the journey – and of the creative process. We adventure from A – with the honest intention of arriving at B – but somehow find ourselves

281

winding up at K, having stalled at W and rested at P, explored a few digits out of curiosity and knocked over a few punctuation marks en route.

Regrettably, it's human nature to want to seek to justify why *best-laid plans went wrong* and then repackage the story. If we are able to give form to the chaos, we demonstrate control over time and space. Some of us even create books that assert the notion that K was, in fact, where we intended to be all along. *I Cycled Into The Arctic Circle* is a case in point: so, too, perhaps, is *The Bible*[13].

Above all, what matters is that *a journey was made*. It's a failure of courage to deny our relative helplessness and like Greene, my own book is an attempt to reveal, in honest detail, what went wrong: to show that it's ok to be *only human*. That's all we need to do: bear witness.

Duthie undertook a tough, physical, extroverted peregrination through unfamiliar lands and languages, hampered by adverse weather, blood-sucking insects, bombed-out suburbs, pipe-smokers, brownish-black bread, the Ungodly and inadequate French machine tooling.

In the making of the film and this book, I, too, have made a peregrination, one that has been every bit as perilous, haphazard, daunting and exhausting as that of my hardy muse. I propelled myself carelessly, fearlessly, following introverted alleyways into my own heart, into a place of unresolved troubles, all knotted over with weeds of anxiety, self-doubt and clumsily misplaced feelings of guilt. I spent years in that place they call *Development Hell*[14], although Purgatory[15] – that waiting room crowded with the almost good, the also ran, the B team and the nominee – perhaps describes it better. Purgatory perpetuates what Nietzsche[16] cheerfully described as the cruelest of emotions – *hope*.[17]

On the morning of May 7th 1951, setting off from (A), Duthie would have been incredulous to learn that weeks down the line his final destination was going to be the Arctic Circle (K), and not (B) Morocco at all. In early 2000, I'd have been amazed to learn that by the end of this journey made in tribute to a deceased deaf Aberdeenshire cyclist, I would find myself living in a pumpkin patch in China. Who'd have thought it? *Ni hao*.

As far as I know Jim never reached the Middle Kingdom[18] but I've no doubt at all that he would have leapt at the chance. I do sometimes ponder as I set off on my rickety bicycle into Beijing's thronging streets: *who is really steering this thing?*

Arguably, above all, Jim has been my truest companion these past 15 years, ushering me onwards with timely blasts of off-shore breezes and the occasional buttery[19], his steely and persistent Belger eye-in-the-sky urging that I fulfill the mission: for him, for his people, for myself – and for all those I dragged so mercilessly along for the ride.

But now Jim, it's time for a parting of ways: *The End of the Affair.*
Yours aye, Matt.[20]

PS: As I was completing this letter, the cheap-looking telephone at the café bar started ringing. The proprietor picked up, listened, nodded and offered me the receiver at the end of its coiled, quivering cable. *"Hello?"* It was Vicky, about to turn in for the night. I'd purposefully not brought my cell phone out with me but this did not deter her. I assured her I was ok, and was staying for another drink; perhaps a beer. I then read aloud these parting words, adapted from the closing sentences of Greene's novel, part of Bendrix's bitter prayer to a God he blames squarely for his misery:

O Jim, You've done enough.
You've robbed me of enough.
I'm too tired and old to learn to love.
Leave me alone forever.

1. Cocktail typically made with, among other ingredients, tequila, vodka, light rum, triple sec, and gin. It is so named because of the resemblance to the colour and taste of iced tea. There is some dispute as to the origin of the concoction. A slightly different drink is claimed to have been invented in the 1920s during Prohibition, by a certain "Old Man Bishop" in a local community named Long Island in Kingsport, Tennessee. The drink was perfected by Ransom Bishop, Old Man Bishop's son. In 1972 Robert "Rosebud" Butt claims to have invented the drink as an entry in a contest to create a new cocktail including Triple Sec while he worked at the Oak Beach Inn on Long Island, NY. Various local New York references echo Butt's claims. The drink has a much higher alcohol concentration (approximately 22 percent) than most highball drinks due to the relatively small amount of mixer. Long Islands can be ordered "extra long", which further increases the alcohol to mixer ratio.
2. In April 2011 Hulse worked briefly in Bristol with Alan Brown on animated projections for his brother Toby's play for *Oxford Playhouse* about aviation pioneers the Wright Brothers. They stayed at Ruth Pendragon's one-bedroom flat, Alan taking 'the proper bed'. In October 2011, in the chaotic months following his hasty departure from a life with Lucy Brown and Tippy (see p.151) in Edinburgh, Hulse crash-landed in Bristol. He lived partly at Ruth's and partly

in a one-room artist's studio on Park Street. On his arrival, Ruth had labelled the bedroom as *Alain's Room*. The French spelling is a reference to Alain Muny, a character in the BBC TV Second World War drama *The Secret Army* (1977–79). Muny is resistance organisation Lifeline's wireless operator, representing wily cunning, independence and guile.

3. English novelist and author regarded as one of the greatest writers of the 20th century.

4. Set in London during and just after the Second World War, the 1951 novel examines the obsessions, jealousy and discernments within the relationships between three central characters: writer Maurice Bendrix; Sarah Miles; and her husband, civil servant Henry Miles. Greene's own affair with Lady Catherine Walston played into the basis for *The End of the Affair*.

5. Hulse and Pendragon share a distaste of materialism and the mere existence of objects. Once, when a tower of CDs clattered in their plastic cases to the ground, Pendragon exclaimed: *I just cannot bear the bloody intransigence of things!*

6. The edition of *The End of the Affair* Hulse discovered was published by Vintage in 2003; here he is picturing the cover of the first edition, published by William Heinemann Ltd in 1951.

7. 平方: one-storey dwelling within a hutong neighbourhood.

8. The *Swallows and Amazons* series by English author Arthur Ransome was first published in 1930. Central protagonists include John, Susan, Titty and Roger Walker (Swallows) as well as Nancy and Peggy Blackett (Amazons) and also uncle Jim, commonly referred to as Captain Flint.

9. Pop vocal duo from the UK, consisting of David Van Day and Canadian-born Thereza Bazar.

10. Play on lines from the T. S. Eliot poem *The Love Song of J. Alfred Prufrock* (1920): *Is it perfume from a dress/That makes me so digress?* And: *I grow old … I grow old/I shall wear the bottoms of my trousers rolled.*

11. *"The United States and Great Britain are two countries separated by a common language."* A saying that has been widely attributed to George Bernard Shaw, beginning in the 1940s, e.g. *Reader's Digest* (November 1942), although it is not found in his published works.

12. More wordplay, from William Butler Yeats' poem *The Second Coming* (1919): *Things fall apart; the centre cannot hold; Mere anarchy is loosed upon the world …*

13. *"An ancient novel full of murder, corruption, homosexuality, bestiality, incest and cruelty. It is often read to children on Sunday."* The Canadian Information Minister (2003) urbandictionary.com

14. In media industry jargon, development hell is a state during which a film or other project remains in development without progressing to production. A film, video game, television program, screenplay, computer programme, concept, or idea stranded in development hell takes an especially long time to

start production, or never does. Projects in development hell are not officially cancelled, but work on them slows or stops.

15. Purgatory, according to Catholic Church doctrine, is an intermediate state after physical death in which those destined for heaven undergo purification, so as to achieve the holiness necessary to enter the joy of heaven. Only those who die in the state of grace but have not in life reached a sufficient level of holiness can be in Purgatory, and therefore no one in Purgatory will remain forever in that state – or go to hell.

16. German philosopher, cultural critic, poet, composer, Latin and Greek scholar. He wrote several critical texts on religion, morality, contemporary culture, philosophy, and science, displaying a fondness for metaphor and irony.

17. *"Hope is the worst of evils, for it prolongs the torment of man."*

18. A translation of the Mandarin name for China – *Zhōngguó*.

19. A roll – or *rowie* – originally made for the fishermen sailing from Aberdeen's harbour. They needed a roll that would not become stale during the two weeks or more that they were at sea. The high fat content meant the rolls also provided an immediate energy source.

20. Email messages submitted via website *dummyjim.com* are forwarded to Matt Hulse. On behalf of and in the spirit of deceased author James Duthie, he responds, always signing of with the words *Yours aye, Jim*. Such exchanges have been occurring quietly behind the scenes since 2008. Hulse attributes the sign-off to his friend John Moffat.

SELECTED MESSAGES
Sent To *dummyjim.com* 2008–2015

Hello Dummy Jim, I think I am a little late with my message. I believe your trip has ended. What a pleasure it was to read about your travels on this beautifully put together website. Thank you for sharing your wonderful experiences. I look forward to hearing about your future adventures! All the best, Briony.

Dear Briony. You are very far from a little late. 'Better to start in the evening than not at all'. Do you cycle much yourself? Yours aye, Jim.

You're full of wise words! I cycle whenever I can, it makes me feel really free, like I could just take off anywhere. I want to do a coast to coast trip in Summer. Your website in excellent. I love the short films from each city. Did you film them yourself? Looks like it was filmed on a Super 8? Looking forward to hearing from you, Best, Briony.

Dear Briony. On a long journey I contemplate. Perhaps some wisdom grows in these times of silence. Aye, the filming was on Super 8mm, but it is original material, not archive. It is wonderful how little things have changed over time - although perhaps the placement of a simple frame makes one look afresh at a tired subject. I favour symmetry. Yours aye, Jim.

Mr. D. Jim, what a disarming and intimate website! I've never seen one like it. I am presently forwarding the link to a whole slew of pals, all different. Like a rare book, I think this site will appeal to them for different reasons. It's so specific, yet universal. Thank you for the brilliant work thus far. Best, Doug.

Dear Jim. How long did it take you to plan your route? What time limit did you plan and how many miles a day? Have you stuck to a plan or deviated, by accident or on purpose? Excellent pedalling, keep it up. Regards Marion.

Dear Marion. They say chance favours a prepared mind. I am always well prepared and have been able to take advantage of chance opportunities and accidents. As you may know I was originally intending to get to Morocco, but certain technical problems meant that I ended up pedalling to the Arctic Circle. I accept this outcome. Yours aye, Jim.

Dear Dummy Jim. I am unsure as to whether this is an email address where Matt Hulse can be reached but I was hoping to make contact with him in relation to the film project about the cyclist James Duthie. I am an assistant to a producer who is curious to learn a bit more about the project. Is there a treatment or script yet for the film? Regards, 'X'.

Dear 'X'. Thank you for your message. I shall leave a note for Matt on the signpost at the crossroads. It is likely that he will spot this on his way to, or from, town, unless he is in a terrible flap. Yours aye, Jim.

Dear Jim. Dream light, pedal tight. Osaka.

Dear Osaka. Certainly whenever possible I have dreamed lightly, sometimes having visions of great weightlessness, when all the troubles of my journey are over, the ride is smooth, I need not pedal any longer. No decisions are necessary. In other dreams I am simply passing through. No one sees me. Or I am wearing the wrong clothes, or worse, I am naked. What is the point of this journey? Pedalling tight is necessary only uphill or in the narrow streets of Amsterdam. However I am fine and I thank you for your concern. Yours aye, Jim.

Hey Dummy Jim! Come on, don't be tired! Love, Gappy Jim.

Dear Gappy Jim. What an interesting and funny name you have! Do people tease you and call you gappy? Jokes are meant well but can sometimes be a wee bit cruel. I shall try not to be tired but I have cycled many, many miles to get this far. Perhaps I simply need a cup of hot coffee, a cold shower or a dip in a loch. Do you have any ideas of how I might stay awake? Otherwise I may cycle asleep into the Arctic Circle and damage it, or worse, fall in and … well, who knows where the Circle ends? Yours aye, Jim.

Dear Nicola. Thank you for your Kindly support. Your finger-spelling tea towel will be dispatched once I have returned from a journey by bike to Kirkintilloch to retrieve some butter. I expect this irksome peregrination to take up the best part of a week. Please keep your dishes wet for the time being. Yours aye, Jim.

Dear Jim. I am doing a report for my American Sign Language class in the USA. I stumbled on your site and enjoyed it so much. You have done an awesome job on this. Thank you, in my report I made it my favorite Deaf-related site. Debby.

Dear Jim. I liked cycling along with you very much in the mid of the night recovering from a bronchitis. Nicole.

Dear Nicole. Bronchitis! My Goodness. That is quite serious. Thank you for managing to pedal alongside despite your condition. You have been very brave indeed. I hope you are feeling a little better now? Did you manage to reach the Arctic Circle? How was it? Were you cured? Yours aye, Jim.

Jim … you can do it! Adventures are always worth it. Kind regards, Sam.

Dear Sam. Some adventures take longer than others. This is only natural. One must hope that there is some benefit in length. Would the world's great bridges have been constructed if the engineers' imagination did not exceed their common sense? I am mindful however of the mighty railway bridge at Dundee, arching over the silvery Tay, and how this led to disaster in 1879. Which shall be remembered for a very long time. Yours aye, Jim.

Dear Jim. On your birthday we showed your short film called God Gives Nuts But Does Not Crack Them to a group of 7–9 year old Beijing school children and told them your story. They said they liked the different languages (BSL and French) but that it was too too short. Their favourite thing was the music. From Vicky.

Dear Vicky. Thank you. This is a transcendent and beautiful notion. Yours aye, Jim.

Good morning. I am a teacher at the University of Specialist Deaf Education. I'm from Saudi Arabia, Riyadh City. I have two sisters, deaf. And the website is beautiful and orderly. I want the world to recognize that deaf people are smart. But I have some questions, allow me? Meead.

Dear Meaad. I would be happy to answer your questions. Yours aye, Jim.

Ok, thanks Dummy. I'm really happy with this. What is the latest phase in the study has been completed? What is the cause of deafness you have? I know American Sign Language, Arabic and I hope that I know sign language Scotland. Are you married? I love you so much. Meaad.

Dear Jim. Seeds do not grow in their packets. Aloma.

Dear Aloma. As you have picked up, I am rather partial to the occasional proverb. I appreciate that seeds do not grow in their packets. I have had some bulbs from a trip to Holland, at the back of the airing cupboard, beside the winter socks, and these have not stirred at all. I shall get around to planting these in the spring. As for my own growth, I have been out of the packet for quite some time now. I think I may have fallen on barren soil to start with, but the Kindly Folk are helping me flourish. All I need is a little watering, to reach my potential. Do you know any one with a hose? Or a watering can? Even an old tin cup of water will help. Yours aye, Jim.

Dear Jim. Keep going! your website is a joy. Emma Zing.

Dear Emma. What a fantastic surname you have. Does it cheer you up, every day? Thank you for your encouraging comment. Do not worry, I am bound to keep going, in fact now it would be impossible to stop; huge momentum has been built up over the years. Or perhaps someone has tampered with my brakes. I have no fear. I shall simply aim my bike at a comfortable place. Yours aye, Jim.

I think this is wonderful, magic and even silver!! Samantha.

Your website is fabulously engaging! The Dummy Jim story sounds intriguing and your approach to the film sounds equally wonderful. I'm an ASL interpreter in Rochester, NY, where we have a HUGE deaf population. I am sure this film will make a big splash in the Deaf world, and hopefully in the hearing one as well. Bravo for striving to make a Deaf story that will be resonant for Deaf people, and not "Hollywood-ized"! We do have a Deaf film fest in this town, the next which will happen in 2011. Hopefully Dummy Jim will be finished by that time and can make an appearance there. Cheers! Kimberly S. Kelstone, CI/CT, Staff Interpreter, National Center for Deaf Health Research (NCDHR)

Dear Jim. Hello - but you died years ago, lol. Mail sent by 'undefined'.

Dear Jim. Well done! Nearly there. Heidi.

Dear Heidi. Indeed, I have nearly completed my epic voyage. The problem of course is that the final strokes of the pedal do seem to take the most effort, do you not agree? In addition, the Arctic Circle is in fact a moveable feast, currently drifting northwards at the rate of about 15m per year. Yours aye, Jim.

Very original and funny but still interesting and finally very clever and nice. In short way: I can sign: GREAT! Karel Redlich.

the path is beautiful & pleasant & joyful & familiar (Meister Eckhart). Buck up little camper ;) Double kisses, double hugs. Daisy.

Good show. Keep it up. I'm anxious to see the Arctic Circle in Norway. I've been to 66–33 N. on a motorcycle, but you are taking the bold way. Martin Falk.

I buy my pal what? Wig. Also by worms why? For fish. Caleb have yo yo. He make string for self, use spider web not yarn. I have pet wolf name Caleb. It love van ride. It stare my x-ray. It think bones real. Caleb Perry.

Keep going, you're nearly there. The Irish are screaming for ya! Niamh.

Dear Jim, you are taking us on such a fine journey and cheered me up so much, please rest well but continue the story. thank for your travels, gaylie x

Hey…here's your message of encouragement. I saw about this site on BBC news and it's so cool. I'm currently trying to sleep off my lunch before I go out and have dinner at 7pm and this is keeping me so pre-occupied I really don't think it's going to happen. On a really random note I used to work with children and young people who signed and I always hate that since I'm not using it I'll forget stuff (though I still always find myself signing "thank you" all the time…at least it seems I'm keep-ing my manners (and I can still ask for tea and biscuits) anyway, it has made me feel strangely happy that I could pick up some of the things you where saying. Ok, such a good site. Good work! Chris Boyce.

Stop being a lazy bam and go. Greg.

Hello, I'm deaf 25 years old from Los Angeles, USA. I'm coming to Europe this Summer of 2009 to explore in London, France, and many countries. Can you bring me information about deaf community in Europe. Thanks. Joseph.

Dear Jim. i am sorry i haven't written in a while. i have been very busy but also suffering from consumption and therefore a bad cough. I know that fish are important to you so i thought you would appreciate this piece of writing by Ivor Cutler which mentions both fish and cough. It is called fish professor. "having spent 8 years trying to teach his pet herring to cough but without success, a perverse ichthyologist went out and bought a lungfish and a box of Havanas." Best wishes, Deirdre.[1] ps. well done with being shortlisted for the Helen Keller Award.

1. Artist Deirdre Nelson's innovative approach to community art practice was of significant inspiration in the making of Dummy Jim.

Walk the dog in the cold air. Ailsa.

Rest well, pedal hard and think of what it will feel like when you have finished your great project. Amanda Game.

Would it be agreeable to you if I were to embed the Dummy Jim trailer on the official Grateful Dead[1] website forum - dead.net? I've been aware of Dummy Jim's website for a while now but not until this rather grey, forlorn looking morn' did I immerse myself in its contents. It's encouraged a gentle fit of effervescence! Inspiring, homely, warm and enveloping, arousing the senses like space dust on the tongue. It has also nudged me towards the pantry: a Dundee Cake[2] beckons.

1. American rock band formed in 1965 in Palo Alto, California. Ranging from quintet to septet, the band was known for a unique and eclectic style, which fused elements of rock, folk, bluegrass, blues, reggae, country, improvisational jazz, psychedelia, space rock and for live performances of lengthy instrumental jams. In the early 1980's - in the midst of a hippy phase – Hulse asked his uncle Phil Brown for a cassette recording of the band. His uncle replied: "No. I don't want to see another generation of Dead Heads." Instead Phil home-taped a C90 cassette for his nephew (thus killing music), with The Human League's 'Dare' on the A side and a compilation on the flip, including tracks from

Bauhaus, Gang of Four, The Birthday Party, A Certain Ratio and Joy Division.
2. Traditional Scottish fruit cake with a rich flavor, often made with currants, sultanas and almonds; sometimes, fruit peel may be added. It originated in nineteenth-century Scotland, and was mass-produced by the marmalade company Keiller's.

Arbeit hat bittere Wurzeln, aber suesse Fruechte! It's a saying of mine. Keep going, Jim, and pedal hard. Yours aye, Svenja.

Dear Jim, with great pleasure I have been travelling your website - so many things to see and do! Also I am very happy that you succeeded in crossing the german border, because sometimes this turns out to be obstaculous. Me myself, I also had the chance to travel a bit with my work: this autumn I spent in beautiful Galicia, shooting an even more beautiful movie but be careful, i am covered again, this time as a Wehrmacht Officer. So, my dear friend, stop snorting, get your bones up and hit the pedal! Greetings from Berlin, Oli Bigalke.[1]

1. Actor Oli Bigalke was cast as a German border guard during the Moonstone Filmmakers' Lab in 2006.

fear not jim, you're almost there now … and the best is yet to come. When you reach the arctic circle, it's worth the trip. But always remember my favourite saying, the journey is the destination. Oh, and another favourite, A little of what you fancy does you good, oh, and Misery loves company. I could go on, but I'll stop there. This is the best thing I've ever seen online. Thank you for sharing. Lucy May Schofield.

Get some rest Dummy jim, you must be very exhausted after all this riding. SM Crago

Dear SM Crago. It has been an exhausting journey, this cannot be denied. Rest has been a wee bit hard to muster. Travel broadened my mind and heart and I am still dealing with its deep and lasting impressions. A new world unfurled on that road and it won't very well fit back onto my old map. Yours aye, Jim.

"A new world unfurled on that road and it won't very well fit back onto my old map." What a wonderful sentence. Thank you. SM Crago.

This afternoon I saw your feature film Dummy Jim at the IFFR (big screening at Pathé 4); I enjoyed it very much. Last year I cycled to John O´ Groats – Land´s End Tour. Started at Orkney and then via the Scottish North-West Coast and the Western Isles down Southwards. Your movie brings back a lot of sweet memories! And I must admit: there´s no better country as Scotland. Martin Koopmans (50) The Netherlands.

Dear Jim. I'm so happy to hear that your journey is almost over and that your story will be told to the world at last. Well done for keeping going even when times were tough and friends seemed too far away. You were always in our hearts. Love Sandie x

Dear Sandie. This is a very nice message to receive, thank you. The film has just been completed and of course there is a strange sense of 'gap'. However I know a thing or two about bridge building. There have indeed been some very tough times, the like of which I never could have imagined, and friends certainly were far away. It is reassuring to know that I was carried in folks' hearts. Yours aye, Jim.

jimmy ma' boy … focus on your goal, lad. focus on your saddle and spokes. focus on your green-eyed beauty. focus on your circle of latitude with gratitude. and may those bonny iced cakes wrap their arms upon your return. Randall.

Dearest Jim. My bicycle tours will mean more when I have you with me. Yours, Gretchen.

Hello! I am sorry to trouble you. My husband wants to do a report on 'I Cycled Into The Arctic Circle' for his American Sign Language course. He says the story has inspired him. Unfortunately, we live in the United

States and cannot find a copy of the book here. I have found two online, but both were over $100, which we cannot afford. Margaret.

Dear Margaret. I am pleased that your husband has chosen to do a report on James Duthie's book. Certainly it has inspired us too. Yes, the cost of these books has shot up since we started activity with the film – to ridiculous levels. I have a suggestion. I would be happy to spend time in the local library and make a complete photocopy of the journal for you, and mail it over. Yours aye, Jim.

I never expected this evening to contain such amusing and inspirational work. The world has taken on a brighter hue. Good on you. Gabrielle.

Anonymous message sent from the USA:
heyyyyy!!!!!! keep calm and carry on. eat lots of bananas! jim me old boy how re you. you are scotish. im not but i can do a sick scotish acent. well keep goin but dont stop for nothing not even for hagess lol. hay dude keep going cause you wont mack it. no you will go go gog gog gog then go home and see you mum. Your MUM in BED. im joking lol. chick dippers. lol lol mum im scared lol dad im scared rofl. hello i have your kids. i will kill you.

Dear Jim. Just finish it off! Jack.

Drink milk responsibly. The Broon.

LIST OF PLATES

Several of the plates and page include hand-written commentaries. These were devised by Matt Hulse and Nick Currey, and penned by the latter. The childrens' drawings are reproduced by kind permission of Inverallochy School, Invercairn, Scotland.

Considerable effort has been made to attribute copyright where necessary, but there may be errors. We apologise for any apparent negligence.

Omissions, corrections and any other matters may be brought to our attention. After being viewed with scepticism and considerable irritation, valid points will be noted for amendment in any future editions of this masterful, learned work.

p.1 Personal note from James Duthie found in the 1957 paperback edition of his journal.

p.2 Photograph by John Fraser Studio, Fraserburgh, Scotland.

p.10 A facsimile of the original photograph chosen by James Duthie for the first edition of *I Cycled Into The Arctic Circle* (1955); photographer unknown.

p.13 Photograph by John Fraser Studio, Fraserburgh, Scotland.

p.15 Maxine Homal.

p.17 Richie Buchan.

p.19 Jack Cowe.

p.21 Michaela Barraclough.

p.24 Michaela Barraclough.

p.25 Cairnbulg beach. Top middle – Matt Hulse, Jeni Reid and Ian Dodds make it up as they go along. Bottom middle – Matt Hulse brandishes a Nikon R10 Super 8mm camera; Ian Dodds prefers the more sophisticated Canon 5D. Meanwhile Samuel Dore salutes imaginary companions. Photographs courtesy of Ailsa McWhinnie (squarepictures.net).

p.27 Photograph by Ruth Pendragon, in the style of *RECIPE COOK BOOK by Madeline on Meals: For a more healthier way of life.*

p.29 AJ Roy.

p.31 Emma Masson.

p.33 Preparatory sketch by Nick Currey for BSL finger spelling tea towels. In braille: *The Lord Bless The Blind.*

p.35 *Cobbler Learning to Make Shoes, Training School for Deaf Mutes, Sulphur, Oklahoma, April 1917.* Hine, Lewis Wickes, 1874–1940, photographer. From the records of the National Child Labor Committee (U.S.), Library of Congress Prints and Photographs Division Washington, D.C. 20540 USA. Licensed under Public

Domain via Wikimedia Commons. No known restrictions on publication.

p.37 Jack Cowe.

p.40–41 Disused fishermen's net-drying poles viewed from the lantern room of the Fraserburgh Lighthouse Museum. Photograph by Ian Dodds featuring Samuel Dore.

p.43 *Teaching a Deaf-Mute to Talk, Training School for Deaf Mutes, Sulphur, Oklahoma, April 1917.* Hine, Lewis Wickes, 1874–1940, photographer. From the records of the National Child Labor Committee (U.S.), Library of Congress Prints and Photographs Division Washington, D.C. 20540 USA. Licensed under Public Domain via Wikimedia Commons. No known restrictions on publication.

p.45 *Dummy Jim Ice Cream: A Recipe From Flanders* by Jan van Os (Brasschaat, Belgium). Ingredients: 3 egg yolks, 110g real Scottish fudge (chopped or broken into small pieces), 250ml (whole) milk (depends on your diet), 200ml whipping cream. Preparation: Beat the egg yolks and the fudge until white, smooth and frothy. Add the milk, stirring constantly. Whip the cream until almost stiff. Add it to the egg mixture. Make sure that all ingredients are thoroughly mixed. Put the mixture in an ice cream maker for 45 minutes. Or, if you haven't got a machine, put the mixture in a shallow bowl then in the freezer for 30 minutes. Get it out and whisk firmly, then put it back in the freezer for 30 minutes. Repeat until the ice cream is smooth and without crystals in it. Enjoy!

p.47–49 The shore at Fraserburgh, viewed from the lantern room of the Fraserburgh Lighthouse Museum. Photograph by Ian Dodds featuring Samuel Dore.

p.52–53 *Rotterdam, Laurenskerk, na Bombardement Van Mei 1940.* Unknown. Licensed under Public Domain via Wikimedia Commons.

p.55 Photograph of Matt Hulse and Tishna Molla by Fotostudio Kissfish, Volendam, Holland. On Hulse's return to Scotland – after an exploratory trip retracing Duthie's route – a copy of the paperback edition of Duthie's *I Cycled Into The Arctic Circle* (1957) that the director had ordered online was waiting for him. On its cover, an image of Duthie taken in 1951, also in Volendam, dressed as a Dutch fisherman.

p.57 AJ Roy.

p.59 Photograph of Svenja Würm by Gudmund Årseth. Würm and Årseth operated a photo booth during the community coffee morning at Invercairn Community Hall on Saturday 14th May 2011.

p.62–63 Michelle Finnie.

p.66–67 Photograph of Samuel Dore by Ian Dodds.

p.69 Emma Bartlett, Edinburgh, 22nd May 2011. Over several months Ruth Nichol photographed dozens of her friends and colleagues displaying cards with individual words from proverbs that appeared in the *Dummy Jim* screenplay.

p.71 *Amalienborg Palace in Wonderful Copenhagen* (SAS Scandinavian Airlines). Licensed under Public Domain via Wikimedia Commons.

p.73 Illustration by Nick Currey.

p.75 '*Scotland gets its brains from the herring*' is a quotation from Ivor Cutler's

I CYCLED INTO THE ARCTIC CIRCLE

Life In A Scotch Sitting Room, Vol.2. Episode 6. It first appeared on the 1976 LP *Jammy Smears* (Virgin Records). An early draft of the *Dummy Jim* screenplay included a scene set in a fish canning factory called *Cutler's,* based on the famous *Maconochie's* (Fraserburgh) where James Duthie worked. David Bowie was slated to play a cameo as the factory foreman, primarily in order that Lucy Brown could finally meet – and potentially kiss – the singer. The label – designed by Nick Currey – later used for a1950's style advertisement, animated by AnneMarie Walsh.

p.77 Nick Currey's hand-drawn design for the BSL fingerspelling tea towels.

p.79 *The Seal-Hunter, Noatak (1929).* Curtis, Edward S., 1868–1952, photographer. Licensed under Public Domain via Wikimedia Commons. No known restrictions on publication.

p.81 Detail from a 1951 tourist guide to holiday motoring in Sweden.

p.83 Extract from Matt Hulse's screenplay for *Dummy Jim* (2007), developed with assistance from the UK Film Council, Scottish Screen and Moonstone International. The chorus mimics the doggerel of poet William McGonagall.

p.85 Photograph by Alex South and Oliver Rundell (Sweden, 2010).

p.87 Advertisement (detail) from a 1951 tourist guide to holiday motoring in Sweden, purchased online by Matt Hulse. *The Nordiska: The Number One Department Store of Stockholm … Complete … High Class.*

p.89 *Tennisstadion,* Stockholm (1942) Andersson, (SvD) Stockholmskällan. Licensed under Public Domain via Wikimedia Commons.

p.91 Lucy Brown aboard the Norwegian cruiser *Hurtigruten* ("the Express Route"), a daily passenger and freight shipping service along Norway's north western coast between Bergen and Kirkenes. Towards the end of their tour of Sweden and Norway (October 2002), having skidded hundreds of kilometres along snowy, icy mountain roads – and despite having seen multiple adverts for studded tyres promoted by a company called *Viking* – Hulse and Brown decided to divert to Bødo, where they would join the Hurtigruten, thus cunningly leapfrogging their planned road trip southwards through Norway to Trondheim. Hulse was at the wheel as they approached the centre of Bødo. The articulated truck in front of them slowed as it approached a busy roundabout. Braking, Hulse took the vehicle into a skid and quickly wrote-off the hire car in the subsequent (serious) head-on collision. As the pair slid towards their unknown fate, Hulse turned to Brown: *I'm sorry, but I think we're going in.* Brown (bracing herself against the imminent impact) replied: *That's ok.* It's true what they say: hours seemed to pass. A burly Norwegian truck driver with naturally-purple cheeks appeared at the shattered driver-side window. He pointed at the tyres: *You need Viking.* Suffering from shock and whiplash, the pair used the coastal voyage as a chance to recover, eating biscuits and drinking cheap red wine – about all they could afford.

p.93 Photograph by Samuel Dore of traditional Scottish stovies, oatcakes and – not pictured, because Dore cannot stand it – fresh beetroot, served on location at the Mintlaw Café (Scotland).

p.95 Michelle Finnie.

p.97 Emanuel Swedenborg. Stipple engraving by C & A Paos. Licensed under CC BY 4.0 via Wikimedia Commons. wellcomeimages.org

p.100–101 *Crowded Dormitory (One Wall), Training School for Deaf Mutes, Sulphur, Oklahoma, April 1917.* Hine, Lewis Wickes, 1874–1940, photographer. From the records of the National Child Labor Committee (U.S.), Library of Congress Prints and Photographs Division, Washington, D.C. 20540 USA. Licensed under Public Domain via Wikimedia Commons. No known restrictions on publication.

p.103 *Imolo Samuel – Blind – and Sister, Congo, c. 1900–1915.* Reproduced with thanks to the Regions Beyond Missionary Union Archives, Centre For The Study of World Christianity, University of Edinburgh.

p.105 Michael Finnie.

p.107 James Duthie on the front page of the Örnsköldsvik Allehanda (detail), Friday 15th June 1951. *Deaf and Dumb Scotsman Bikes Through Europe.*

p.109 Cairnbulg beach. Matt Hulse braces his thighs to help stabilize Ian Dodds as he films Sarah Kenchington piecing together her kinetic musical instrument sculptures. Photographs courtesy of Ailsa McWhinnie (squarepictures.net).

p.112–113 Robert 'Bobby' Stephen in Cairnbulg Gospel Hall. Photograph by Ian Dodds.

p.115 Jack Cowe.

p.117 Illustration by Nick Currey for the website *dummyjim.com.*

p.119 O.H. von Lode – Leem, Knud (1767). *Beskrivelse over Finnmarkens Lapper, deres Tungemaal, Levemaade og forrige Afgudsdyrkelse* (Copenhagen: 1767). Public domain.

p.121 Detail of a 1920's print engraving purchased by Matt Hulse on eBay.

p.123 Sarah Kenchington performing live at Dovecot Studios (Edinburgh) on the 13th November 2009. Photograph by Gudmund Årseth.

p.125 *Louyre*, Fougax-et-Barineuf, Ariege (France). At a certain stage during the writing of the *Dummy Jim* screenplay, Hulse lit - *and inhaled smoke from* – a long hand-rolled cigarette containing marijuana, home-grown by a man in a plaid shirt, living at the top of a nearby mountain. At what point did the drug take effect?

p.127 Page (detail) from the *Fredhøis*, a Norwegian summer holiday magazine published by Fredhøis Forlag, purchased by Matt Hulse and Lucy Brown during their Scandinavian tour (October 2002).

p.130–131 *Mountain Sami People, Lyngen, Norway.* Postcard. Photograph by T. Høegh (1928). Licensed under CC BY-SA 3.0 via Wikimedia Commons.

p.133 *Badstuga. Acerbis Travels, Nordisk Familjebok.* Licensed under Public Domain via Wikimedia Commons.

p.135 Norwegian summer holiday magazine published by Fredhøis Forlag, purchased by Matt Hulse and Lucy Brown on their Scandinavian tour (October 2002).

p.137 View of the North Sea from the shore at Cairnbulg. Photographs courtesy of Ailsa McWhinnie (squarepictures.net).

p.139 Detail from the *Fredhøis*, a Norwegian summer holiday magazine published by Fredhøis Forlag, purchased by Matt Hulse and Lucy Brown during their Scandinavian tour (October 2002).

p.142–143 Detail of a 1920's print engraving purchased online by Matt Hulse. 'We'll pay for it' references Alastair Reid's poem *Scotland*.

p.146–147 Samuel Dore in Cairnbulg Gospel Hall, photographed by Ian Dodds.

p.149 Samuel Dore photographed by Mary McFeeley.

p.151 Jack Bryce.

p.153 Advertisement for a restaurant (detail) from a 1951 tourist guide to holiday motoring in Sweden, purchased online by Matt Hulse.

p.156–157 An early sketch of Nick Currey's made during discussions on the possible use of maps to help illustrate Duthie's journey.

p.159 Film props. Period pocket watch sourced by watchmaker Robert Trueman.

p.161 Detail from the *Fredhøis*, a Norwegian summer holiday magazine published by Fredhøis Forlag, purchased by Matt Hulse and Lucy Brown during their Scandinavian tour (October 2002).

p.163 Lauryn Masson.

p.165 Gudmund Årseth, photographed by Svenja Würm.

p.167 Samuel Dore at the launch of *dummyjim.com*, 23rd August 2008, Centre for Contemporary Art, Glasgow. Photograph by Gudmund Årseth.

p.170–171 Rock carving from the Bronze Age (Sweden). Public domain image from avrosys.nu.

p.173 *Edward Miner Gallaudet* by Mathew Brady. From the Brady-Handy Photograph Collection, Library of Congress Prints and Photographs Division Washington, D.C. 20540 USA. Licensed under Public Domain via Wikimedia Commons. No known restrictions on publication.

p.176–177 Sami drum from Åsele Lappmark. Frame drum. 50x34 cm. No.13 in Ernst Manker's *Die lappische Zaubertrommel* (1938/1950).

p.179 *Dog Smoking (19th January 1923)*. National Photo Company Collection, Library of Congress Prints and Photographs Division, Washington, D.C. 20540 USA. Licensed under Public Domain via Wikimedia Commons. No known restrictions on publication.

p.181 British Deaf News, July 2013. Photograph by Ian Dodds.

p.183 A J Roy.

p.185 *Seagulls Hovering Hopefully as the Norwegian Fishermen in Scotland Gut Fish Ready for the Market* (1941–1943). Licensed under Public Domain via Wikimedia Commons. No known restrictions on publication.

p.187 Joy Buchan, Broadsea, Fraserburgh (2005). Photograph by Matt Hulse.

p.189 Jake Hasson.

p.192–193 (detail) *Kampieren No.15 "Het Ochtendbad"*. Postcard purchased online by Matt Hulse, stamped in Haarlem (NL) 6th May 1937. No message.

p.195 *Native Girls, Marken Island, Holland* (1890–1900). Detroit Publishing Co., catalogue J, foreign section. Library of Congress Prints and Photographs Division, Washington, D.C. 20540 USA. Licensed under Public Domain via Wikimedia

Commons. No known restrictions on publication.

p.198–199 *Language Is The Whole People.* L–R: Nille Hannes, Jan van Os and Matt Hulse. Out of shot, Joost van Veen. Photograph by Lucy Brown, Antwerp, Belgium, July 2010.

p.202–203 Photograph sent by Alan Brown to Matt Hulse during his time in Wilmington, NC, USA (2012). The original hand-written message on the back of the photograph reads: *June 1960. Just arrived on the border. Other side of board is "Welcome to Bonnie Scotland."*

p.206–207 Illustration by Nick Currey charting Hulse's 12-year journey towards the completion of *Dummy Jim.* An animated version of the same image features on the *Dummy Jim Special Edition DVD* as an extra with the title *Making Of.*

p.210–211 Beach at Cairnbulg. Matt Hulse and Gabriel Foster Prior mishandle the tent in advance of a shoot.

p.212 *Fallen Girders, Tay Bridge* by Board of Trade. From the National Library of Scotland's digital gallery. Licensed under Public Domain via Wikimedia Commons. No known restrictions on publication. The Tay Bridge disaster occurred during a violent storm (11 on the Beaufort scale) on 28 December 1879 when the bridge collapsed while a train was passing over it from Wormit to Dundee, killing all 75 people aboard. The bridge – designed by Sir Thomas Bouch – used lattice girders supported by iron piers, with cast iron columns and wrought iron cross-bracing. Bouch had sought expert advice on 'wind loading' when designing a proposed rail bridge over the Firth of Forth; as a result of that advice he made no explicit allowance for wind loading in the design of the Tay Bridge. There were other flaws in design, maintenance, and in quality control of castings, all of which were, at least in part, Bouch's responsibility. Bouch died within the year, his reputation as an engineer ruined. Bouch's design for the Forth Bridge was not used.

p.213 *Tay Bridge from South After Accident* by Board of Trade. From the National Library of Scotland's digital gallery. Licensed under Public Domain via Wikimedia Commons. No known restrictions on publication. *The Tay Bridge Disaster* is a poem written in 1880 by the Scottish poet William McGonagall, who has been widely 'acclaimed' as the worst poet in history. It ends:

> *Oh! ill-fated Bridge of the Silv'ry Tay,*
> *I must now conclude my lay*
> *By telling the world fearlessly without the least dismay,*
> *That your central girders would not have given way,*
> *At least many sensible men do say,*
> *Had they been supported on each side with buttresses,*
> *At least many sensible men confesses,*
> *For the stronger we our houses do build,*
> *The less chance we have of being killed.*

Full poem: mcgonagall-online.org.uk

p.218–219 Illustration by Nick Currey, originally for *dummyjim.com.*

p.232 Photograph by John Currey (Rauhaniemi Beach, Tampere, Finland).

Eveni

No. 27,204 (EST 1879)

N.E. CY-

Mr JAMES DUTHIE

DEAF mute Mr James Dut[hie] 41 Main Street, Cairnb[u] who travelled thousands [of] miles round the world by mot[or-] cycle and motor-scooter, a[nd] wrote a book on his exp[eri]ences, died in Stracathro H[os]pital today from injuries received after an accident [on] his motor-scooter.

Mr Duthie was rushed to h[os]pital last night with he[ad] injuries after being thro[wn] from his scooter while driv[ing] towards Laurencekirk on

IST DIES AFTER
OAD ACCIDENT

in-Laurencekirk road. No vehicle was involved.

Duthie (44), a deaf mute childhood, achieved fame cclamation when his book, ycled Into the Arctic " was published, describ- 10,000-mile cycle tour he made in 1951.

only £12 he had travelled through France, Belgium, Holland, Germany, Denmark, Norway and Sweden, then North to beyond the Arctic Circle.

It was in 1960 that Mr Duthie made his biggest trip when he covered some 14,000 miles through 15 different countries on his motor-scooter.

BACKWARDS
On the Making and the Made

Gareth Evans

In light of all that's happened in this book so far, and despite the various forms of joy conveyed and experienced by one's meeting with its content, comment, design, paper, binding and image fecundity, it is important to remember that, unless major alterations are made to the machine in question, it is not possible to cycle backwards; and even then, it would be notably unadvisable.

Do not try this at home; do not try it away from home either, since close encounters with forward-moving white vans, HGVs and other monstrosities of the highway will not be aided by counter-pedalling.

That said, the will, or desire, inherent in the very idea that it might be possible to attempt such a venture, is of course fully present in this magnificent volume and all the attendant activities radiating in the manner of fine spokes from its central axis.

Rarely has this correspondent come across an enterprise in which such generous affection is so palpable, so evident. Care. Attention. Love for all that is made – objects, people, living things, the world.

The camera that gazes; the hands that make, that assemble; the weave of self and selves, the common ground of the shared undertaking.

This era seeks a culture of capital as its primary expression. The *Dummy Jim* project declares itself instead a capital of culture, an open field, a welcoming shelter and a fresh cartography towards a wholly different means of being in the world.

It knows the edges of the map are central. It knows time is on its side and it takes its needed time, a whisky of production, distilling its loyalty. It knows despair is not an option.

And so, given all of this, the resounding call must be: not forwards, not backwards, but onwards!

Gareth Evans is a writer, presenter, producer and curator.